Collectible TEAPOTS

A Reference and Price Guide

Tina M. Carter

Published by

krause
publications
The World's Largest Hobby & Collectibles Publisher

Please, call or write us for our free catalog of antiques and collectibles publications. To place an order or receive our free catalog, call 800-258-0929. For editorial comment and further information, use our regular business telephone at (715) 445-2214.

ISBN: 1-58221-018-7
Printed in the United States of America

Dedication

To God be the glory.
"God has given each of us the ability to do certain things well." Romans 12:6 L.B.

Acknowledgments

First and foremost, I thank my husband and family who are always supportive of my teapot ventures: Jerry, Justin, Kevin, Jeff, Becca and the many foster youth whove made our house their home.

This book would not be possible without all of the wonderful teapot and tea time enthusiasts Ive had the opportunity to correspond with, talk to and meet over the years. I wish we could have one big tea party and bring our favorite pot!

A special thanks to tea time friend, Paul "Angel" Moreno, who got to read this manuscript in the rough stages with her well-known honesty. Many collectors allowed me to photograph their teapot or use their teapot photo (their names are listed with each photo caption). A special mention to an internet friend, Suze Richmond, for lending me teapots and sending encouraging e-mail. Thank you to Gary Stotsky for sharing his wealth of information and photos of his collection.

Thank you to the delightful people who purchased my first teapot book and the many who prompted me to write this one with price guide information

I lift my teapot to pour your cup! Enjoy!

Table of Contents

The Teapots

Introduction

Tea time is ready with this teal lustre teaset, made in Japan, c1930s-40s; tea strainer with porcelain base made in England; tea cozy to keep the pot warm, c1950s; and a tea caddy spoon to measure the tea advertising Salada Team. The tea set and eight cups, saucers and dessert plates are valued at $95. The rolling tea cart with inlaid floral design, possibly made in Italy, is worth $300.

When you have one special teapot, it's meant for sentimental treasuring. If you have two teapots, surely one is meant for tea. However, three teapots (or more) are the beginnings of a collection. Whether you've only begun collecting teapots or you've enjoyed them for many years, you've come to the right place to help identify, find values and care for these vessels of tea time.

Sidney Smith (1771-1845) is quoted as writing: "Thank God for tea! What would the world do without tea?" I say, what would tea be without the teapot? Would tea have ever been so popular without the diverse teapot in which to brew the flavorful leaves? I think not, and the proof is in the thousands of teapot collectors worldwide.

While coffee has vied for the lead in hot beverages, especially during the 20th century, tea has been steadily faithful to provide what no other substance can claim; it soothes and stimulates in an amazing contradiction. Some studies now show that green tea may have anti-cancer agents. No wonder tea has found quite a resurgence of popularity in the last 15 years of the 20th century. With this renewed interest in drinking tea has come a varied and practical array of modern teapots. Many modern teapots couldn't produce a pot of good tea if they tried, while the fine china section of retail stores exhibit a teapot to match almost any open-stock line.

Tea shops have opened all around the country. Most are small and quaint with a plethora of pots to choose from along with bulk tea and an assortment of accessories. Other shops serve tea with a variety of menus to choose from. One company has spawned the collectibility of teapots with a passion: The Collector's Teapot. This mail order company features an amazing selection of teapots from pure whimsy to practical Brown Betty's and everything in-between. (See "Reference" chapter for more information)

Today you can purchase hand-painted teapots similar to one your great-grandmother had or a conversation piece in a bust of Abraham Lincoln. Many companies have reissued heirloom patterns and styles knowing that collectors abound. One such example is the recent popularity of chintz-decorated china. The Royal Winton Grimwades company in England has reissued many of its chintz items, including teapots. The Spode company has continued to produce many of its blue-and-white patterns, including one similar to Blue Willow, called "Spode's Tower."

With this growing popularity of tea drinking and teapots, a heightened awareness of vintage teapots has emerged. Antiques and collectibles dealers realize that collectors are hunting for teapots and tea-related items. Unfortunately, examples from the 1800s have become increasingly hard to find. Vintage pots from the late-1700s to the 1880s are more often found in museums and publicly owned collections.

The Unique Teapot

Teapots demonstrate a unique charm, evoking a sense of simpler times, the respite with friends or family and even revisiting Victorian pleasures. The characteristic handle, spout and body of a beautiful pot has smitten even those who don't collect. The fact that a teapot brews a flavorful refreshment only adds to the appeal. Collector tastes are as varied as the availability of teapots. Many delight in imaginative and futuristic teapots of artistic creation. Other collectors relate to a fond reminiscence, favorite hues or teapots depicting an era.

Grasping the handle of a teapot Whether enthusiasts realize it or not, each part of a teapot is subjectively representative. The ideal teapot has a handle designed for a firm grip when pouring the pot of steaming tea. Not unlike the handle we would like to have on life—plenty of room yet confident, sure and in control. The person pouring tea has control of the situation—unless he or she happens to be the server and not involved in tea time. The best handles allow for room to grip without knuckles touching a hot pot. Many teapots have been designed with a helpful thumb grip and indentations for fingers.

The drippy spout of a teapot The spout of a teapot has gone through a variety of changes through the years. Spouts of a 1700s English teapot resembled the beak of a bird; those of a Chinese Canton pot had demure openings; and Japanese teapots breathed steam from dragon figured spouts. Victorian tea time in the 1800s demanded a spout which poured smoothly without drips or sputters. Cutting away of the upper

portion of the spout aided in this matter along with ingenious attempts such as a down-turned spout or a self-pouring teapot by which a plunger pushed the tea out a spout resembling a faucet.

The spout of a teapot symbolizes the serving of tea, the pouring atmosphere of relaxing tea time. In this seemingly age-old tradition, pouring of oneself during intimate conversation or gossipy whisperings are often just as refreshing as the tea and crumpets. A gesture of hospitality lies in the lifting of a teapot for just a spot more tea. Collectors would agree, whether they take tea or not, that it's almost impossible to gaze upon a teapot without imagining tea pouring through the spout, into a cup.

Rounding the body of a teapot   The body of a teapot is happily stuck between the firm grip of a handle and the flowing spout. Designers and artists have endeavored to work this portion of a teapot in a marriage of form and function. The challenge has always been to create a body that will brew an even flavored pot of tea while appealing to trends of the era. Modern figural teapots have ventured to extremes of pure whimsy without much consideration for brewing of tea, so much so that labels or boxes should state "For decorative purposes only." Tea enthusiasts will agree the world over that the round bodied teapot, such as the English Brown Betty or tiny Yixing, brew the best tea.

Figural teapots have been produced almost since the very evolution of teapots. Small Chinese teapots revealed the integration of nature into their art. Teapots bore twig handles and finials or were shaped like the well-known lotus flower. Both early Chinese and Japanese teapots incorporated dragon designs. By the time tea drinking and teapots reached Great Britain, the many figural and varied bodies of a teapot were copied by English potteries.

Whatever the social status of tea drinking, the hostess must have a teapot that showcases her unique taste. The smooth lines of Art Deco can be just as appealing as the footed Victorian rococo teapot with applied flowers and detailed hand-painted designs. A bulbous copper-clad teapot beckons you to touch nearly as much as an ornate silver chased set. The collector's hand reaches for the colorful textures of majolica just as quickly as the matte-finished pottery teapot.

The next time you try to explain your enjoyment of teapots, just pick one of the three elements: handle, spout or body. Then proceed to tell how they're wonderfully fashioned, practically shaped or simply brew the best pot of tea.

Generalist or Specialist?

When I began collecting teapots 18 years ago, I thought, "There must be others who think teapots are as wonderful as I do." I was right. Other collectors had been gathering teapots long before I started a newsletter to network enthusiasts. So many collectors inquired about a book or reference for their collection that I knew I must discontinue the newsletter for a much needed book. You are now holding the second book I've written for those who treasure teapots as much as I.

I began my love for teapots in much the same way you may have — someone gave me a teapot. I was given a common moss rose teapot which had belonged to a great aunt and after placing it on the fireplace mantel I knew I wanted to find more. My mom gave me a couple others she'd had for a long time; from then on I watched for teapots at every swap meet, antique store or yard sale. I'm often asked how many teapots I have. Who has time to count? I estimate my collection encompasses approximately 850 teapots, which includes about 400 miniature or small souvenir teapots.

A collection doesn't have to be nearly as large to be enjoyable. Then again, there are teapot collectors whose acquisitions number beyond mine. A few people collect as an investment but the majority simply revel in the hunt, excitement of the latest find and, more often, the chance to tell others about their gleanings.

The most enjoyable teapots are usually those with a story. It may be the way they were found or the right price paid. The most cherished teapots are heirlooms or those with sentimental value. Their monetary value may be low, but the owner considers the teapot priceless.

Generalist collectors   Collectors fall into one of two categories: generalists or specialists. Generalists collect a variety of teapots according to personal appeal or price range. This type of collecting is fulfilling because the wider range allows for frequent acquisitions. The drawback may be that you soon find some of your teapots no longer hold your interest and you'll need to weed out the less desirables. Give each addition to your collection a due amount of consideration.

Education is also a key to ensure generalist collectors don't become easily dismayed with previous purchases. If you can identify teapots from many different eras, you'll come away satisfied more often than not.

Specialist collectors Specialist collectors focus on a specific category and search out those teapots meeting criteria of a certain manufacturer, type of composition, color or size. On occasion, specialists may be tempted to purchase an item outside their chosen category. Most enjoy the challenge of a narrow field and the hunt for elusive teapots within that range. One such collector has set her sights on Meissen teapots, which are not only scarce but priced into the thousands of dollars. Her collection is not large but well-planned and exquisite.

Hall China teapot collectors comprise a popular specialist category. The vast number, style and color of Hall teapots made since the 1930s to the present make this possible. Enthusiasts often search for all the decorated examples of a particular shape.

Other specialist categories include figurals, English teapots, miniatures, Chintz china or American pottery styles. While specialists focus on one area, generalists often find they have "collections within their collection." An example would be souvenir teapots which can easily grow into a separate collection. Whether you concentrate your collection endeavors on one area or you enjoy teapots in general, you'll be continually amazed at the wide variety of styles, shapes and colors produced through the years.

Teapots as an Investment

If you want a fast return on your investment, teapots may not be the way to go. But the market value for teapots has steadily increased, especially with recent popularity and the growing antique and collectible information field. Those who truly collect for investment purposes are specializing in rare teapots or those with values into the thousands of dollars. You may have to be patient to sell for a profit, giving time for the market to adjust. Investors will do better by commissioning their wares with an auction house such as Christie's or Sotheby's.

On a smaller scale, check antique publications for auction companies. Many list the items they are dealing with or even have photos. This will give you an idea if your teapot investment is something they will work to secure the best price.

Striking the Right Deal

Almost every person with a large collection has been tempted to become a dealer out of sheer necessity. Becoming a dealer is a another subject, and there are good books and helpful people if you're truly headed in that direction. At some point in collecting, you may find that you are dealing or working with dealers. I encourage both buyers and sellers that the goal is for both to feel satisfied in the end.

Remember that the dealer or seller is hoping to make a nice profit. Antique dealers have overhead costs to pay not to mention the work of securing, cleaning and recording their wares. Dealers, if you want to move your teapots, think about what collectors might realistically pay. I recommend that dealers set a certain profit percentage that they use across-the-board when pricing items. Should research tell you that a teapot is worth $85, and you paid $20, would you rather price it at 100% profit at $40 and have it sell, or price it at the book price of $85 and have it stay on the shelf for a year?

Even though you may have a price in mind that you'll pay for a teapot, I believe it's unfair for potential buyers to set a price. The seller is essentially asking you to price their item. You won't know if you'll be offensive or pay far too much. It is the seller's job to research the item, if possible, and decide on a price. Get the seller to give you at least a starting point. I've passed up some interesting teapots because I felt the seller needed to give me an idea of what kind of price he wanted. Even if I know something about teapots, it's not right for me to price an item that I'm going to buy. I'd like to price it low every time, wouldn't you?

The best reason to collect anything, including teapots, is for personal pleasure. Have fun researching your teapots, learning the differences between pottery, porcelain or pewter and silverplate. Find out the stories behind the teapot you're about to buy so you can share it with someone else. Search for the perfect pot for brewing your own tea. Collect teapots because they have a unique charm all their own and the leave profit-making to the dealers. Time for a 'cuppa!

How to Use This Book

This book is for you. Here's what you'll find: Whether you enjoy one special heirloom teapot or you have a continuing collection, you've come to the right place. Welcome to the world of lovely and unique teapots! Take a moment to scan the whole book. Look at the Table of Contents so that you have a general idea of what you'll find. I encourage you to use this book rather than allow it to collect dust (let your teapots do that for you!).

When reading the text, don't forget to peruse the Glossary. Like other antique and collectible fields, there are some terms specific to teapot collecting. In referencing the various eras, both the century designation (20th century) and actual numbers are used (1800s). For example, the 1800s is the 19th century and the 1900s is the 20th century and so on.

Bookmark your favorite sections. Use a highlighter to mark information about specific teapots or subjects. There's nothing more frustrating than knowing you read something but can't find it. If you don't want to mark up this book, buy another copy. Use one for reference and to take with you on your teapot hunts and keep the other for the coffee table.

Finding Your Teapot in this Book

If you want to find information on a specific teapot, the first place to look is in the Index. There you will find teapots described in various ways. To make things easy, I've often given a teapot a name which may also describe the pot. For example, to find a duck-shaped teapot, first look for "Duck."

Other teapots will be listed by their manufacturer name such as "Hall China Co." You may have to try two or three places in the Index to find a particular teapot. Don't give up. If your teapot is not in this book, you may be able to find one that is similar. Is there a term in the Glossary that might help you find your teapot? An example may be "Lustre" and you hadn't realized your teapot's glaze was actually lustre.

Although there are about 900 teapots shown in this book and an additional 500 in the price guide listings, your teapot may not be within these pages. That's the wonderful paradox of collecting teapots: Thousands of styles have been produced in the last 200 years, making teapots a challenge to collect. Many teapots have no known written reference.

Once you've checked the Index, try looking at the photos in the category for which your teapot falls. If you're not sure, you may have to view a couple sections. A floral decorated bone china teapot could appear under the chapter on Floral teapots or the chapter on China. Another place to check is with the many teapots described in the price listing under each category although there may not be a photo available.

What's It Worth?

The value of any given object is what the buyer is willing to pay. Everyone wants to get the best price for their treasures while buyers want to feel they are getting a deal. No matter which end of the transaction you're on, remember that prices in this guide are just that—a guide. If you buy or sell somewhere within 20 percent of the values in this book, satisfaction is on your side.

The values in the book are given for teapots considered to be in excellent condition: no chips, cracks, crazing; no tea stains, scorched bottoms or glued parts. Teapots without a lid are worth very little and this price guide assumes the teapot has a lid. If the teapot you are researching has any of the above flaws, the value must be reduced. The greater the type of damage, the more it will decrease the value. A small nick on the inner rim, which does not show when lid is in place, will not reduce the value as much as a noticeable chip on the end of the spout.

Prices in this guide represent the value you would expect to see should you find the same teapot in an antique shop. The value of an object is often a subjective thing determined by many factors, including sentimental value and personal appeal. To determine some type of basis, I've used antique shop prices as a benchmark. To our frustration or delight, depending upon the region of the United States, prices will vary for the same exact pot. Collectible prices are generally higher on the East- and West Coasts and lower in the Central- and Mid Regions of the United States. Prices in this guide reflect an average or general range of the entire United States.

Other guidelines I've used to price teapots include published prices from auctions, magazines and antique and collectible periodicals, other price guides and reference guides. Last but not least, I've used the prices I've recently paid for teapots along with the prices other people tell me they've paid.

There will always be the sensational sale of some teapot for a previously unheard of amount. Unless the authenticity of a rare and antique teapot has been verified by either an appraiser or a documented reference, be careful about the prices you hear about. It takes years for the investment value of most teapots to increase; even to double. Don't buy as an investment unless you've done your research and possibly even paid an appraiser.

Buy what you can afford, collect for personal enjoyment, sell for a reasonable profit and teapots will bring you many years of pleasure.

Pictures (and Captions) Tell the Story

Teapots of various categories have been used to illustrate the text of this book. For the best source of information on a particular teapot, refer to the specific category. Illustrations for sections under "The Teapots" will be representative of that category. Photo captions include a brief description and the approximate market value of each teapot, but the text will describe many of these same teapots in detail. Don't rely solely on the captions; read through the text, also.

The approximate era a teapot was made will be listed when possible. The notation "c." stands for *circa*; in antique circles, this denotes 10 years either side of the date given but I use this determination more often for five years on either side of the date given. Most teapots were produced for many years and only modern collectibles have been limited editions.

You will find the term "modern" used throughout this book (and with the photo descriptions). I decided this is the best way to describe teapots made from 1980 through the year 2000. The exact year a teapot was made is not always possible to pinpoint, but, in the 20th century, each decade has items that were popular during that era. A different twist on materials, methods of production, decoration and styles help determine what era a teapot may have been made.

Tea Master two-spouted tea pot by Hall China has two chambers for hot water and tea. The brochure that accompanied the pot explained its use. It was marketed by the Twinspout Pottery Company of New York in the 1940s. This teapot in cobalt is an especially desirable color, with a value of $175.

Collector's Guidelines

Starting a Teapot Collection

New collectors will find 20th century teapots still attainable with modern examples prevalent. But beware! One teapot can easily lead to a collection of hundreds because new tea shops, gift and department stores, plus antique shops, swap meets and flea markets, are displaying teapots.

Most vintage teapots available today range from the 1930s-1950s. Teapots made from 1890 to 1920 have become harder to find but may show up on occasion at an estate sale or at an auction company. Be ready to pay anywhere from several hundred to thousands of dollars, depending upon the verified age of these teapots. You may want some form of authenticity, such as an official appraisal or at least time to research a mark, before making an expensive purchase. Teapots from the 1700s and early- to mid-1800s are predominantly found in museums or privately owned public collections. It's recommended that any collector frequent museums to get a feel for these older examples.

As you begin to peruse the selections, there are some care and handling tips that will help. The manufacturer mark tells us much about a pot, but it's most frequently on the bottom. Be sure to hold the lid of a teapot with one hand while taking a peak under the pot. I often cradle the lid between my pointer and index fingers as I lift the teapot with the other hand, preventing the lid from accidentally slipping off. Many teapot lids have been made to hook or lock on, but others have a heavy lid that just seems to unexpectedly fall off. When enjoying tea time, it's also a good practice to keep a couple fingers on the lid finial while pouring tea. Most teapots are made to be picked up with the handle, but use caution for older, delicate pieces. Watch for any cracks in the handle that may sug-

gest it could break or crack further.

The lid of a teapot should always be wrapped separate from the body (i.e., after purchasing a teapot shipping or storage). When unwrapping, do it over a soft area, such as a couch or bed, in case the lid should drop out of the packaging. Should you want to store some teapots in boxes, I highly recommend the flip-top plastic storage boxes available at department stores. Bubble wrap is the best wrapping material. Retrieval will be much easier if you list the actual teapots in the box on a label or piece of paper. I also recommend using duct tape across the top of the box where the two pieces of the lid come together. If you need to tip the box when storing, it will prevent the lid from accidentally coming open and spilling out your treasures.

Teapots should not be stored in extreme temperatures. If your attic freezes in the winter or sweats in the summer, this is not the place for teapots. Extreme temperatures can cause crazing and even breakage either when in storage or after removal.

Another extreme to be aware of has to do with tea time—always warm the pot with hot water from your tap before filling with boiling water. Many a teapot is crazed because of the shock of boiling water added to a room temperature or cold teapot.

What to Watch For

For any teapot that draws your interest, examine it closely for cracks, crazing or chips. Sometimes the smallest little chip can go unnoticed. Run your fingers around edges to feel for chips. Get to know the various types of pottery, porcelain and china so that you'll know a reproduction from a 1940s teapot. Hand-painted detail, whether under the glaze or added after firing, tells a lot about the quality and period of a piece. Modern, inexpensive teapots often have detail applied before firing and the quality is quick, inaccurate or oddly placed.

This Wade teapot missing its lid is perfect for holding pens and pencils. This teapot is part of a set of two teapots: one for tea and one for water (on a tray). The mark dates this pot from the 1920s. This pot, without the lid and as only part of the set, is a $20 item.

No matter if it's old or new, finer teapots will have painted design applied in an amazingly accurate and detailed fashion.

New collectors should try to avoid the enthusiastic approach of buying every affordable teapot they find. While this will help your collection grow, it won't be long before you need to weed out those pots which you find inferior or less desirable. Consider a focus for your collection and be selective. At the same time, consider this recommendation for purchasing any antique and collectible: If you are really attracted to an item and it's within your budget, buy it. It may be gone tomorrow. Many a collector can attest to a time or two when they left to "think about" a purchase, only to return and find it was gone.

One of the litmus tests when considering the addition of an item to your collection, is if it evokes some sentimental feeling or reminds you of an era for which you have fond remembrances. For example, if a teapot reminds you of something your grandmother used to have or something you played with as a child, buy it. If you can relate to the teapot in some way and are deliberating, chances are you should make the purchase instead of being disappointed when it's gone later.

Teapot Condition

One of the dilemmas presented in collecting teapots is that lids are prone to falling off and breaking. A teapot without a lid is nearly worthless and there are only a few reasons to purchase one:

- ✦ You want to use it as a flower pot or some other practicality
- ✦ It has some identification to aid you with a similar teapot
- ✦ It has sentimental value in some way

It is possible to find a lid, but it may take years. Other times a marriage is made: a lid from a different teapot or sugar bowl will fit your lidless teapot. In most cases, this marriage of lid and pot will be noticeable and possibly not very appealing. Before purchasing a lidless teapot for more than $10, give it much consideration.

Most teapots are utilitarian in form and thus subject to the wear that comes with use. The most common sign of wear is crazing. Crazing is the fine cracking in the glaze of a teapot and may be present on the inside, the outer glaze or both. This cracking happens primarily because the glaze has not fused

properly to the body. Porcelain producing companies have long dealt with this problem and have worked hard to invent the right chemical combination of glaze and porcelain body which fuse as one to prevent crazing. One pottery that has succeeded is the Hall China Company, leading to the durability and popularity of its teapots. I have never seen a Hall China teapot with crazing, though it would be possible if an inferior piece slipped through.

Crazing on the inside of a teapot does not detract from the value as much as crazing on the outside. Inside, the fine cracks may be stained brown if tea was brewed in the pot. There are several ways crazing is caused:

- ✦ A teapot was dropped or bumped
- ✦ It has been exposed to extreme temperatures
- ✦ It may slowly appear over time, although crazing is not a sign of age or that a teapot is antique
- ✦ When fired in the kiln, the body and glaze expanded and contracted at different rates

The teapot value should be reduced anywhere from 10% to 20%, depending on the amount of crazing.

Another inherent type of damage or wear on a teapot is chipping. The spout of a teapot is prone to chipping. Some chips are quite small and barely noticeable and really don't devalue the pot. Another common place for chips is on the inner rim or under the lid—the place where these two areas come together and are easily bumped. While a chip under the lid or rim may not show, depending upon the size of the chip, the value is reduced 10% to 20%.

Teapots are prone to cracking; this usually comes from being dropped or harshly bumped. To determine whether a crack is all the way through or just some crazing, look to see if the crack shows up on both the inside and outside. You may also need to fill the pot with some tepid water to check for leaking. If it leaks, it cannot be used for brewing tea. Even if it doesn't initially leak, it's possible that it would with hot water or that the crack would spread once hot water was added to the pot. While some cracks do not readily show in display, the value should be lowered by 30%.

Age, Price and Origin

The best way to determine the age of a teapot is to know the various types of wares. American pottery and porcelain teapots are quite distinct compared to English china and porcelain. Japanese decoration has a representative type of styling, scenery and people. Purchase at least one book of marks and continue to add to your reference library, as well as your teapots. You may find you only use a few pages out of a book but they may be invaluable for identification of teapots. I have several books showing antique teapots. I've never been able to find one of those old teapots, but by perusing the pages every so often, if I did see one, I would be able to recognize it.

Markings on the bottom of a teapot are one of the best ways to determine whether the teapot is antique, mid-20th century or modern. Should there be no mark, try to find a similar example either in a book or for sale. Some antique stores will allow 24 hours to hold an item so that you can do some research.

Markings also help identify origin. The obvious ones say something like "made in Japan" but others may only have "hand-painted" or some numbers and letters. English teapots often have some numbers or letters hand-painted on the bottom. These were used by the company in-house to determine quality assurance, match lids with pots, identify the pattern or glaze and other parameters.

Teapots made in Japan often have similar stamped marks such as A-183 in type. Lefton and Enesco have used these types of in-house designations. While these marks mean very little to collectors in identifying exactly where a teapot was made, they can help you recognize an English teapot from one made in Japan or the United States.

Manufacturer's Marks

Using the manufacturer mark on the bottom of a teapot is the easiest way to identify age, origin and possible value. Invest in books devoted to marks on pottery, porcelain and silver or pewter. See the Reference section in the back of this book for suggested books on marks.

The manufacturer mark is usually placed on the bottom of a teapot, but the mark or a portion of it can be found under the lid. In the case of Oriental teapots, a mark is often just under the handle. If you don't see a mark on the bottom, take a good look all over the teapot, even under the lid.

From the late-1950s to the 1970s, companies used paper labels as an inexpensive way to mark their wares. By the 1980s, new items were marked

on the bottom, even if a paper label was used. This has caused grief for collectors because paper labels or stickers were readily removed. Teapots with a label intact are considered 20% to 25% higher in value because of this identification.

Another nuance in the marking of teapots are those made by a pottery for another company. Quite often, the marketing company' name was placed on the item, leaving collectors confused about origin. An example is the McCormick teapot produced by the Hall China company. The marking reads "McCormick Co Balto, Banquet Teas" and leads unknowing buyers to believe this pot was made by McCormick. The fact is, it was made by Hall China for McCormick. Another example is the small Salada teapot which is only marked "Salada Tea, made in USA" and made by the Brush McCoy pottery company.

Reproductions

The act of producing something which mimics or copies another item is not a new concept. English pottery and porcelain manufacturers in the 1700s readily copied Oriental designs. This was reversed when Japanese companies began producing teapots with a definite European flair. Predicting marketing trends is an age-old process which has proliferated the varied teapots we relish. A popular example is the Rebekah at the Well teapot. This design was first fashioned in England, possibly by the S. Alcock & Co. in Burslem, England, in the early-1800s or the Rockingham Company run by the Brameld Brothers in Staffordshire, England. This motif of the Biblical character Rebekah has been produced by many companies in Great Britain, the United States and even Japan. The Edwin Bennet pottery of Baltimore is given the greatest credit for a version of this teapot produced in the 1800s, but 14 pottery companies have been documented as having produced this teapot from the 19th into the 20th century. Fortunately for collectors, these teapots are either marked or have slightly varying characteristics. Some Rebekah teapots have the words "Rebekah at the Well" as part of the raised design. These teapots are also somewhat of a crossover between yellow ware and majolica in their styling.

While so many potteries produced the popular Rebekah teapot, their intent was to produce a product that was well-liked yet practical for use.

Backstamp in blue ink on a modern teapot made by Crown Dorset, Staffordshire, England.

Brown Betty-style teapot with a paper sticker: "Ridgeways, England." This sticker is especially interesting because of its teapot shape.

An impressed mark on this teapot made by Sadler, England. Letters in gold are used by the company to determine the style of decoration, glaze or decorator.

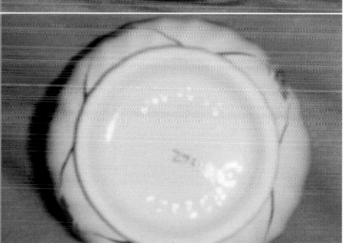

A colorful backstamp on a teapot made by the Harker Pottery Co., U.S.A., which also includes a seal from the Good Housekeeping Institute.

As modern manufacturing techniques have evolved, so has the ability to copy the vintage styles and marks, with intent to pass off something as antique rather than a new version.

Recently, porcelain has appeared on the secondary market with a backstamp similar to those used by many companies in England and the United States. This mark is referred to as the British Coat of Arms mark—a lion and unicorn on their hind legs, holding a shield and topped by a crown. Versions of this mark have the animals standing on a ribbon banner or on leaves. The reproduction pieces only say "Ironstone" and "Victoria" in the shield, although the name "Victoria" is often obscured. No country or pottery indications are made within the mark but a study of similar vintage marks reveals that more information was usually provided; such as "England." These pieces have a celadon background with a heavily decorated blue design mimicking Blue Willow or Flow Blue. The bottom rim of a pitcher or teapot has the typical unglazed portion. This has been blackened by a process attempting to make it look old and used. Collectors need to study types of marks and decoration. In this example, both are quite misleading but can be recognized as modern or reproduced details. (More detail is given under Porcelain teapots.)

During the mid-1990s, a company marketed several styles of children's tea sets in colorful figurals such as a Teddy Bear teaset and Farm tea sets. These sets were marked with paper labels that come off easily. Pieces from these sets are showing up in antique stores. While they may be collectible, they should not demand high prices because original 23-piece sets sold new for approximately $20. (See Children's Teaset section for more detail.)

Other reproductions that collector's need to be aware of are individually commissioned Hall China items such as the Autumn Leaf pattern teapots and remakes of Hull Pottery Little Red Riding Hood. The backstamp differs from vintage pieces, leaving collectors and dealers able to recognize reproductions.

Types of Marks

Backstamp or ink stamp: This type of mark has been applied both under the glaze and over the glaze after firing. Backstamps applied under the final glaze are made permanent with firing, but those done afterwards use a permanent ink or a decal type application. Backstamps were predominantly done in one color of ink into the 1950s. After this time, automated processes made it easier to quickly apply two or three colored marks. Although there are always exceptions, this fact can help in identifying whether a teapot is antique or made between 1960 and the present.

Many well-known companies still use one color of ink for their backstamps but the ink is of a higher quality and often you can actually feel the applied mark. Companies also have the ability to add a lot of information to their backstamps. A popular example is the many shapes and styles of

THE TEA CUP'S FORTUNE TELLING.

Postcard from 1910 depicts using tea leaves to tell one's fortune. Note the Rockingham-style teapot, Rebekah at the Well.

teapots made by the Ellgreave Company, a division of Wood & Sons, England. Its black and red mark is a very detailed shield, including the above information, lions, flowers, stating Ellgreave, three of the Wood's names and dates. Also stated is "Genuine Ironstone."

Impressed or raised marks   Employed as a time-saving and labor-saving method, pottery and porcelain manufacturers have molded their name and country of origin directly into the body of a teapot, predominantly on the bottom. Teapots made in England, the United States and Japan have used this method mainly from 1920 through the present. Marks impressed into the teapot are generally older than those with raised markings. One problem with this method is that a heavy glaze can obliterate the mark. This is one of those times where finding a similar teapot, or a photo of one, can help identify the manufacturer.

Paper labels or stickers   This method of identification is a modern practice used from the late-1950s to the present. Some stickers are quite detailed with gold and applied to the body of the teapot. Others are simply the name "Japan" in a tiny little label applied either to the bottom or side of the teapot. Paper labels are an advertising method and some companies are still applying them to their teapots today.

Hand-written initials or numbers   Hand-written designations as part of the mark are usually done for in-house use and each company may have different reasons and codes. Teapots with a signature of the designer or artist demand higher prices. Examples would be Sasha Brastoff, California or Don Blanding, Vernon Kilns.

Dating Teapots with Backstamp or Mark

While using the mark as your guide to date teapots is one of the best methods, collectors need to gather reference sources to learn about the various marks. Books devoted to manufacturer marks are great sources but so are books detailing specific companies or styles. An example is Geisha Girl Porcelain by Elyce Litts which includes information on various Japanese pottery areas, old catalog reprints and a helpful section about Japanese and

This teapot is marked with both a backstamp in gold and impressed lettering. It is from one of the teapots made in England to help raise funds during World War II. This mark includes the Staffordshire Knot, which has been used by many companies in many versions.

Mark stamped into the base of an aluminum teapot. Made by Sona Ware, The Aluminum Works, Stratford-on-Avon, England.

English language markings.

Teapot companies change their marks over the years and using reference guides can help you determine when the mark on your teapot was used. Keep in mind that the years mentioned can vary. The size of a mark may also be an indication of the period a teapot was made. Companies often changed the size or way the same mark was applied during different eras.

Dating methods Many English companies had or have their unique method of dating. Wedgwood used a method of three capital letters from 1860 to 1906. From 1907 to 1916 the code was changed to include a number. After 1930, the month of the year, a potters initial and the last two digits of the year were used. Pieces made since 1980 bear the company's name and the last two digits of the year made. This is an abbreviated description and just one example of how complex it becomes to decipher one company's dating system. The Worcester Company used a coded system along with a mark bearing their name. The Homer Laughlin company of East Liverpool, Ohio, used what they deemed the "Best China Dating System," in which two letters were used to indicate the year, the month and the plant where the item was made.

The method of using English Registry Marks is very useful for determining the age of any pieces bearing this mark in the form of a diamond with a circle on the top and indicators in each corner of the diamond. In the center is a capital R and double underlined d meaning "registered." This mark was predominantly used from 1842 to 1883 and after that date the word registered was used or "Rd. No." followed by a number. This method has been used from 1884 to the present but, unfortunately, Registry Numbers are not used on all teapots made in England. To date a teapot bearing a registered number, find the table of Design Registry Numbers, issued by the Patent Office in London. (See Reference section for *Kovels' New Dictionary of Marks*).

Should you find a mark which uses Roman numerals, you can find a table of numbers in Webster's New Collegiate Dictionary or other dictionaries, under "numbers."

Look in old book stores or in book sections of antique stores for any references on pottery, porcelain, china, silver, pewter, etc. See the Reference section for an old book distributor in England and request a catalog or check out antique book sellers near you. These are all great places to find some out-of-print book. Even if you only identify one teapot, it's well worth the price.

Date included in the mark Whenever a date is included in the mark on a teapot, don't assume this must be when it was made. More often than not, the date is indicating when the company was established. It would be too labor intensive to change the year in a backstamp frequently; this is why coding or register marks were used. The mark stamped into silver or silver-plated teapots often includes "Est." and a date, which indicates when the silversmith was established in business.

Dates included in decoration Commemorative or souvenir teapots often used the date of an event in the decoration of a teapot. Examples include souvenirs for a World's Fair, the U.S. Bicentennial in 1976, Lewis & Clark Centennial of 1905, and coronations or weddings of English royalty. Beware of teapots made to celebrate some event but bearing a vintage date, such as a teapot made by a Canadian pottery to commemorate the battle of Gettysburg. Decoration on the teapot only states Gettysburg, Pa. 1863. This pot was most likely produced for celebrations in 1963 and the type of pottery and glaze are representative of that era; the date 1863 could be misleading to collectors.

Another method of determining the age or origin of a teapot has to do with actual history of the pot. If you know it was Grandma's wedding present, find out what year they were married and you've dated your teapot. Don't hesitate to ask dealers, family or other sellers about what they know. Even the smallest tidbit about your teapot's background is better than nothing. Write down the info and slip it inside the pot.

Caring for Your Collection

Insurance: As your teapot collection continues to grow, there are some practical steps for taking care of these special treasures. One of the first things to consider is homeowner's insurance. Most policies provide a certain percentage of the value of your home for personal property, but they may have exclusions for valuables. Check your policy and talk to your agent.

Whether or not you need insurance, it's a good idea to periodically take photos or videotape your collection. An inventory is also a good idea, but it can be time-consuming. If you're a new collector, it's easier to start now and enter your information into a computer database or spreadsheet program. Keep a copy of the inventory and the video or photos in a safe place, such as a fire-proof safe or safety deposit box. Should damage or theft occur to your home, you'll have evidence of your collection for insurance purposes.

Don't allow solicitors or strangers to view your collection, because you don't know if they're scoping out your home for easy access to valuables. Although thieves usually go for money, guns or jewelry (which can be sold quickly), teapots could also be sold easily at swap meets or flea markets. This type of incident is rare, but it's better to be safe than sorry.

Display cases   The most common way to store and display your collection is within a curio or china cabinet. This keeps teapots from being easily handled by others and dusting to a minimum. In areas where earthquakes are possible, it's suggested that curio or china cabinets be secured to a wall with a strong lead wire. This would allow for cabinet movement in a mild to medium earthquake without the cabinet actually falling over. (In the case of an earthquake where the walls are moving and ceilings falling, just be thankful if no one is injured—most teapots can be replaced, people can't be.) Most furniture and department stores have good selections of curio cabinets.

Child and pet proofing   I started collecting teapots when my children were babies and I can honestly say they've never broken one. I admit that I've broken one and a cat cracked the handle of another. Training young children about breakable things is not always easy, so take precautions if you have young children in your home or little ones who visit often. You may want to get an inexpensive copper kettle or a children's set and designate it as the teapot youngsters can play with when in your home. I have an elephant shaped teapot, sugar and creamer that is not old and I let the kids have tea time with that set. Another idea is to purchase an inexpensive teapot, possibly with some existing damage, for children to play with, knowing that you won't be devastated should they break it. If you enjoy children and pets in your home, then keep your teapots out of reach, and everyone will be happy.

Display shelving   Every room in your home can be accentuated with teapots. Shelving near the ceiling is a popular way to give you ample display space, yet blend with any decor. It's recommended that this type of shelving be installed with a strip of molding along the outer edge. This can prevent a teapot from gradually "walking" towards the edge from normal vibrations and then falling to break. Even a slamming door or hammering on the other side of a wall (preferably to install more shelves for teapots) can cause a favorite pot to fall and break.

Another method to help keep teapots on their

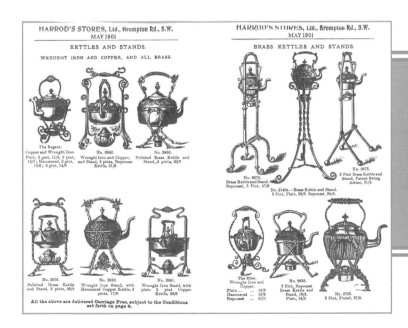

A copy of a 1901 ad from Harrod's Stores in London for brass and copper tea kettles (sometimes called "tipping kettles") with wrought-iron warming stands.

shelves is using the white Stick-Um or "Quake-hold." This pliable material can be applied under pots to keep them in place. This is especially helpful for miniature teapots which tend to "walk" because of their light weight. A fishing line can be used to help keep teapots from falling off shelves. It's done by attaching the line to one end of the wall about at the mid-point of a average sized teapot and bring the line along all of the teapots, to be attached at the other end. The difficulty in this method is when you are moving teapots, you may have to reattach another string.

Making use of your collection You will derive more satisfaction from your collection of teapots when you actually use them. Teapots can enhance any room of your home not only as mere decor items or conversation pieces, but also in practical ways.

Teapots lend themselves well as vases for either dried or fresh cut flowers. If you are going to arrange fresh flowers, you may want to test the teapot to be sure it doesn't leak, even if there are no signs of cracks. On an unusual occasion, the glaze inside a pottery teapot may not have completely sealed the porous clay. Over a period of hours, the water can saturate the clay and cause a ring to appear from the teapot, although you may not notice any true water leaking. Test the pot by filling with tepid water from the tap and leave it to sit for a day. This does not need to be done every time you want to use the same pot but is recommended for each different teapot.

Dried arrangements don't need any special care when displayed in a teapot. This is a great way to make use of a teapot missing it's lid. If the teapot has a floral design or some other pattern, you may want to take it with you when picking out the flowers. It's appealing to display flowers with the same hues found on the pot.

Teapots can be handy storage containers all around the home. In the kitchen, use a teapot to keep cooking utensils accessible or store tea bags. Hunt down teapots in the colors of your kitchen, including wall pockets in the shape of a teapot or teacup. You may also be amazed at the variety of items produced for the kitchen in a teapot shape such as timers, salt and pepper shakers, spoon rests, souvenir or teaspoon holders and even a mini-wind chime. Almost every type of kitchen decoration has been made with a pattern of teapots, such as wallpaper, curtains, paper plates and napkins and tea time accessories.

In the bathroom, use a teapot to store cotton balls, toothbrushes and toothpaste, Q-Tips or other toiletries. It's not recommended to display or store metal teapots in your bathroom because of the continual moisture.

On your desk, keep pencils and pens nearby when stored in a teapot. It's also a great place to store your own stash of candy or other snacks. Individual sized teapots easily store small items such as postage stamps, small change, matches or other miscellaneous items. Some teapots, such as one with a missing lid, have a wide opening where a 4-inch to 6-inch potted plant can be slipped into the opening. Just leave the plant in the plastic pot because teapots don't have the kind of drainage plants need.

Groupings are one of the popular ways to decorate and teapots work well with this method. Gather teapots with a recurring motif, colors and varied sizes to group in a table top arrangement. Remember that an odd number of items are considered artistically appealing. Look for tea-related items to gather with your teapots such as cups and

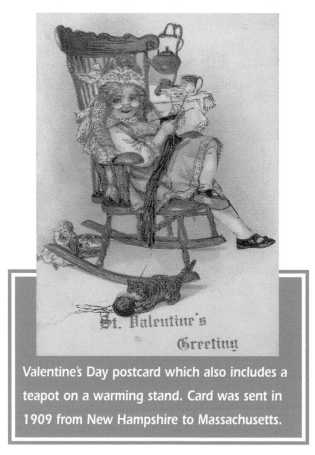

Valentine's Day postcard which also includes a teapot on a warming stand. Card was sent in 1909 from New Hampshire to Massachusetts.

saucers, tea spoons or tea tins. A spray of flowers in one of the teapots will pull your grouping together especially if the bouquet has both similar and contrasting colors. Group three teapots together in almost any available space such as atop the piano, fireplace mantel, bathroom vanity or kitchen nook. This concept works well no matter what type of decor because teapots can be found in Victorian, country, Art Deco, modern and whimsical styles.

Display expensive and vintage teapots behind glass or atop shelves but reserve others for every day use, enjoying your collection all around your home.

Other ways to use your collection While visitors, family and friends will enjoy your collection when it's displayed in your home, you can also offer to lend your collection for public display. Here are some ideas to try:

- ✦ Enter your collection in the local county fair
- ✦ Display it at your local library
- ✦ Exhibit for a club or organization
- ✦ Viewing at a nearby tea shop or antique shop

Safety is an issue at all of the above and you will first need to document exactly which teapots are going to be on display. Give a copy of this inventory to the person you are working with in displaying your teapots. In some cases, you may want to have both parties date and sign in agreement.

Many places have locked glass cabinets for special displays which provide the best security. You will want to make a sign or make sure a sign is displayed noting that your teapots are not for sale. Should you agree to allow a club or organization to view your collection, it may be for just the day and you'll need to be responsible for your items. Take a friend or family member along to help you carry, unload and load and watch your collection. Be ready to make new connections with other teapot enthusiasts.

Teapots were intended for tea One of the most enjoyable ways to use a teapot is to have tea time. If you've never had a tea time before, it's easier than you think. We aren't stuck with tradition today and almost anything is acceptable tea time food, from cookies to croissant sandwiches or fruit and coffee (tea) cake. Tea time with three or four people makes it easier to chat, serve up the tea and have the time long enough to enjoy but

short enough so as not to detract from other things of the day. Tea time can be anytime: morning, lunch time, afternoon or evening. Set a time, invite some friends or family and then plan the menu. Most tea drinkers enjoy a black tea, such as Darjeeling, or green tea (you may want to find out your guests' preferences). But if you want to surprise them, pick up a lightly flavored tea. One of my favorites is called "Celebration Blend" from Fluer de Tea in San Diego. It's a black tea with orange and spices blended enough for flavor but not to be overpowering. There are many fine mail order tea companies and it's fun to try different flavors.

When planning a tea time menu, keep it simple so that you are not exhausted in preparation and can enjoy the fellowship. It's helpful if most of the food can be prepared ahead of time and then all you really have to do is boil the water for tea and set out the tea cups, saucers and flatware. Play instrumental music, light a pretty candle or set out a bouquet of flowers to create a welcoming atmosphere, realizing that tea can be taken in the kitchen, dining room or living room. Tea time doesn't have to be served on delicate china and it's vogue to mix and match patterns. Be prepared to brew at least two pots of tea—in fact you may want to have two kinds of tea steeping in different pots.

There are many good books on tea time to give you interesting ideas but it may help if you have something for your group to focus on other than gossipy news. Reading a poem, a funny anecdote or an interesting newspaper article can be great conversation points.

Tea for special occasions Although some of the most enjoyable tea times are those done impromptu, special occasion teas require more advanced planning. A birthday or Christmas tea require special menu ingredients or washing of a favorite tea set and possibly finding a table favor for each person. This can be as simple as a book mark, special chocolate candy or poem printed on pretty paper. More expensive ideas would be a gift book such as one on tea or teapots, a special cup and saucer to use and then take home or a tea spoon.

Hostessing a tea doesn't require a special occasion, but it will feel like one when you bring out a beautiful teapot, steep some flavorful tea and enjoy a tradition that's been practiced for almost four centuries.

History of Teapots

Had tea never been discovered, perhaps we would sadly be without the wonderful vessel known as the teapot. The discovery of tea is shrouded in legend depending upon which country is claiming tea as their heritage. The most well-known account is of the Chinese Emperor Shen Nung and his peculiarity of having water boiled before drinking. On one occasion, leaves from the Camellia sinensis plant, known today as tea, dropped into his boiling water. Upon tasting this infusion, he found the leaves imparted a pleasurable flavor and had his servants begin to cultivate and nurture the plant. Of course, if the Emperor was using this flavored water, others followed suit.

Another legend has it that the Buddhist who founded the Ch'an School of Buddhism, named Bodhidharma and also known as Daruma, discovered tea. This happened during travel from India to China on his quest of self-imposed seclusion to a cave-temple for nine years of meditation and contemplation. The legend goes that by the fifth year he was fighting drowsiness and meditation was a struggle. In his frustration, he reached for leaves off a nearby bush and began chewing on them. The result was a wakefulness where he was able to continue his contemplation and meditation all because of the leaves from a bush we know as the tea tree.

Another legend tells of how the Buddhist scholar Gan Lu returned to the province of Szechwan from studying in India. With him were tea plants which he planted on Meng Mountain although today there is no proof of tea being first grown in Szechwan but rather in the Yunan Province and from there transplanted into Central China.

Like many other plants, the way the tea tree grows and the types of leaves it produces, change from one climatic area to another. Tea is an evergreen classified in the Camellia family with leathery green leaves. In cultivation, the tree is continually pruned; but left to grow it can reach 60 feet high. The tea bush grows well in low elevation mountains or hills, possibly because of moisture levels.

Once tea began to be cultivated, it was classified with two formal names. One from China called *Thea sinensis* meaning China tea and the other from India called *Thea assamica*, meaning Assam Tea. Then it was dis-

INDIA AND CEYLON TEA — A TEA PICKER.

An advertising postcard for India and Ceylon Tea. A description of how they pick the tea is on the back of card along with a place for dealers to place their name and address. The card was then mailed to potential buyers. This card from Kendallville, IN, 1908.

covered that tea had been introduced from Assam, India to China and the plants were one and same, so it was then classified as Camellia sinensis or China Camellia (from Camellus, derived from a 1700s Moravian Jesuit missionary, Georg Josef Kamel).

While the discovery of infusing tea leaves to flavor water has a long and convoluted history, it's widely accepted that tea was first produced commercially in China. Today it's grown not only in China and India, but other tropical or subtropical regions such as Taiwan, Indonesia, India, Sri Lanka (Ceylon), other parts of Asia, Africa, Russia and South America. Attempts have been made to establish tea growing in the United States, the last about 1920, in southern states. The cost of labor and seasons with insufficient rainfall deterred these efforts.

There are many books which document the varying accounts and legends surrounding the discovery of tea (see Reference Section). Most will have some documentation of the Chinese poet, mystic, scholar and now proclaimed patron saint of tea—Lu Yu. Commissioned by tea merchants of that era, Lu Yu wrote the first book on tea in 780 AD. His writing, the *Ch'a Ching*, or *The Classic of Tea* is a three-volume work consisting of 10 parts wherein tea is described. This included the utensils to be used for preparation and taking of tea and evolved into the Japanese Tea Ceremony. Lu Yu changed the way the world viewed tea and ripples of his writing still touch tea lovers the world over.

Tea Needs a Brewing Vessel

Lu Yu laboriously explained how to brew tea in volume three of his treatise, yet there is no mention of a teapot because it had not been invented. More precisely, what we know as a teapot had not evolved. Tea was steeped and sipped from cups similar in size to those used in Chinese restaurants today, although a much thinner earthenware was used. In accounts of Lu Yu's *Ch'a Ching*: "the cauldron, usually of pig iron, should be smooth inside for easy cleaning...the best and the longest-lasting are of silver" (Woodward, 1980). This cauldron was not a pouring vessel and water was ladled out into cups. Lu Yu also points out that the water should not over-boil and the tea should be frothy when poured into cups. For centuries tea was taken from handleless cups, much like the cups of Lu Yu's writing.

Frothy aside, pouring water into cups presents a challenge without a vessel equipped with a spout or pouring lip. Records of the first use of a pot, resembling a teapot, are obscure, although two theories have been debated for centuries. Many believe that the teapot is actually a modified version of early Chinese wine vessels, while others hold to a thought that the first teapots were actually Islamic coffee pots. Records tell of coffee being drunk as a beverage in Arabia around 600 AD—about the same time as tea was gaining in acceptance, mainly for medicinal purposes. It would still be many centuries before tea would come into its own as a beverage.

The combined idea of a wine vessel and the coffee pot very likely inspired potters and silversmiths to fashion a pot for steeping tea, especially considering that Islamic countries border China. Records of the first use of teapots are from the 17th century when similar ewers had already been formed by Korean potters. The Chinese wine vessel had a straight spout with a small opening and this design can also be found in early teapots. All that was needed for these ewers to be a teapot was a strainer inside to catch the leaves—but that would not be formed until the 17th century.

Chinese Teapots

Records and tradition point to the first teapots being made in China. They were small, similar in size to the handleless cups used for steeping tea. This was not because tea was expensive, for it was grown in China. The process evolved from tea in cups—one for each person—and the individual sized pots made perfect sense. Besides that, tea was not taken in the large quantities we are familiar with in the 20th century.

While the best known Chinese teapots have been produced from the Yixing area, many other potters fashioned unique and durable tea ware. Ornate silver, brass and copper teapots have also been made in China, often bearing dragon motifs and spouts where tea pours through the dragon's mouth. Another decoration often seen on Chinese manufactured teapots is the Buddhistic lion— usually in a sitting position, looking like a bull dog with a beard.

Early teapots are part of what is referred to as Chinese export porcelain and date from about the late-17th century although most pieces in museums or at auction today are from the 18th century. It's said that Marco Polo brought Chinese porcelain to Europe where it was considered to be worth more than gold. Much of this porcelain was from Canton, where it was not only produced, but porcelain from other areas was decorated there and then exported.

The love of blue-and-white china or porcelain can be traced to Canton. Popular patterns from the 18th and 19th centuries incorporate a scene with an island, bridge, trees, mountains, birds, a boat and river. This blue-and-white Chinese export porcelain inspired the Blue Willow pattern of England which has been popular for three centuries. Porcelain produced in Nanking bears a likeness of this blue-and-white design, but differing borders or other detail make it distinguishable. The term Nanking was used by the English in reference to the finest quality Canton ware, although

the two were separate porcelain producing areas.

One of the recognizable styles of Chinese porcelain is Famille Rose. Popular in Europe and the New World during the late-1700s and 1800s, this pattern incorporates a flower into the border of a heavily enamel-painted decoration. Famille rose was done in many variations which included Chinese or Mandarin figures involved in some activity. Other similar patterns have never gained the same attention as Famille Rose.

During the late-1700s and early-1800s, Chinese porcelain qualities changed to become thicker and sometimes flecks of some material are found in the glaze. The Canton Rose and Rose Medallion patterns emerged and production of variations have been produced even to the present. The Rose Medallion pattern is painted with panels of scenes, figures or birds within a solidly detailed background. Chinese porcelain from the late-19th century has been decorated in a pattern called Dragon and Chrysanthemum in an over-all enamel-painted design. When the background is a

This modern Wedgwood Jasperware (unglazed porcelain with decoration in white relief) set includes a creamer and sugar. It is marked: "Wedgwood, England."

rose-toned red, it has been referred to as the Emperor's colors.

The East India Company was founded in 1600 by the Royal Charter of Queen Elizabeth and is considered to be the one of the most powerful economic influences in world trade. It was on this company's ships that tea and Chinese export porcelain, along with spices, silk, art and other items, were transported all over the world. In the New World, the port of Salem (Mass.) was especially influenced by trade from China and one of the few ports not blockaded by the British during the Revolutionary War. In the late-1700s, captains and merchants of this trade were members of a society called the East India Marine Society.

While this society kept journal records of its trade, it also agreed to contribute Orientalia to an ethnological-maritime collection. This collection is held by the Peabody Museum in Salem, endowed by George Peabody in 1867. Viewing this collection and others such as the China Trade Museum in Milton, Mass., presents a glimpse of imported goods from China so popular during the 18th and 19th centuries. Teapots and tea wares were an important part of this trade.

As porcelain and china production was refined, many patterns and styles of both Chinese and Japanese teapots bear similarities. For example, Imari ceramics were produced first in Japan and then in China. There are distinguishable differences which can be referenced such as the glaze colors used and Japanese Imari tends to be heavier.

Reproductions of the above patterns have been made in the 20th century and collectors are advised to study period examples in books and museums. Fine Chinese porcelain is still produced today, affording collectors both modern and vintage teapots examples.

Japanese Teapots

Japan has probably produced and exported more teapots than any other country in the world but was slow to begin this tradition. Tea was introduced to Japan via Buddhists and scholars traveling to China. They returned with seeds and then cultivated tea bushes in the temple gardens. They had taken notice of how the tea service was performed in China. In 794 AD, Kyoto was designated as the capital of Japan and the tea culture which originated in China began to evolve into a form that would be uniquely Japanese. In that same year, the Imperial Palace was built and the Emperor Kammu requested an enclosed tea garden be built as part of the surroundings. During the next reign, Emperor Saga enjoyed tea to the degree that he ordered tea planted in five provinces and an annual tribute was to be held to celebrate the tea ceremony.

Not long after tea's acceptance in Japan, the country met with political and governmental strife and for almost 200 years, shoguns or feudal lords ruled the country while the emperor had very little power. During this time, tea and the tea service were of little importance. By 1191 AD, peace had been regained and tea was reintroduced by a Buddhist again. Abbot Yeisei returned from China with new seeds and has since been called Japan's "father of tea." Again, the area of Kyoto was planted with tea and the small temple garden exists even today. Yeisei believed tea had healing powers and wrote what is dubbed as Japan's first book of tea called Kitcha-Yojoki or Book of Tea Sanitation. Yeisei is quoted in writing: "Our country is full of sickly looking, skinny persons and this is simply because we do not drink tea. Whenever one is in poor spirits, one should drink tea. Drink lots of tea, and one's energy and spirits will be restored to full strength." (Woodward, 1980)

Japan preferred to use tea utensils from China for several centuries. Whether it was romanticized or just convenience, is not known. The formal art of the tea ceremony was perfected and encouraged by Zen priests. The ceremony of drinking tea has two names: Cha-no-yu or "hot water for Tea" and Chado or "the way of tea." Chado's most well-known tea master was Sen-no Rikyu, who encourage a separate tea house with its own path so that there was nothing to distract guests when arriving for Chado. The term used for a tea house is sukiya, meaning "abode of fancy" or "abode of vacancy."

The use of a teapot for tea was possibly introduced to Japan about 1654 by a Chinese priest named Ingen, founder of the Obaku sect of Zen Buddhism. At about the same time, pottery and porcelain production was introduced to Japan by Korean ceramics immigrants. Tea wares were manufactured, including the teapot form. The Japanese, along with Europeans, used teapots for concocting herbal brews used for medicinal purposes. This is a practice that continues today in

Japan, although modern cooking utensils are available.

The use of unglazed earthenware pots became widespread during the 17th century with the evolution of two types of pots. One was a larger teapot called a *dobin* and was used for medicinal infusions or low-grade teas. The other teapot was small, derived from Chinese pots, and called a *kyusu*. These smaller teapots were used for the higher, more expensive grades of tea and are recognizable by their handle attached at a right angle to the spout. If you have ever poured tea from a pot with this handle, you'll realize the practical design and wonder why all teapots haven't been made with just such a handle. The grip is easy and firm while the pouring action seems natural from this angle.

These little pots are produced today in the typical reddish brown, mottled or almost black clay. They are recognizable by their smooth surfaces and incised markings of leaves, flowers, Japanese writing or artistic designs. By the turn of the 19th century, glazes had been added. Some teapots have interesting detail done under a glaze while others are one solid color in a smooth, matte glaze.

A type of ware developed in Japan during the mid to late-1700s has met with some confusion: *Banko*. The first potter to produce a pottery known as Banko was Rozan, a wealthy merchant and amateur potter who marked his ware with either the name Banko (meaning 10,000 or enduring) or *Fueki* (meaning eternal or unchanging). He produced wares, including teapots, after Korean styles. During the 1780s, the Shogun Inyenari heard about Banko and summoned Rozan to the capital, making him the official potter. In this position, Rozan was able to study techniques of the Chinese, and he reproduced Ming Dynasty styles along with Famille Rose and Delft wares. Rozan died at the end of the 18th century.

In 1830, Mori Yesetsu (referred to as Banko II) accidentally found the original Banko formulas containing descriptions of methods of productions along with glazes and enamels. Yesetsu purchased these records and the right to use both marks from the grandson of Rozan (Banko I). Yesetsu and his brother Yohei, who adapted the Fueki seal, produced Banko with a different style than Banko I. The paste like clay used for Banko II ware was thin and translucent with natural colors like white, cream, gray, brown, blue and green. The clay was rolled out very thin. Marbleized clay was made by rolling several colors and then pressing them together, rolling again and then slicing. Banko ware

Advertising card for Lipton Tea shows workers plucking tea leaves. Card has message to remind recipient that a wholesale grocer sells Lipton's teas and to reserve your order. Dated 1909.

PLUCKING · TEA · ON · BUNYAN · ESTATE, CEYLON

LIPTON SERIES.

teapots usually had moveable bail handles which continued part of the design such as twigs or branches. They were decorated with or without glazes, painted, impressed with a design or enameled.

Many Japanese potters began imitating this Banko style causing this name to be used to designate a type of ware rather than one of the two original potters who invented these styles. Banko was recognized as an important pottery style at the 1878 Paris Exhibition where more than 15 Banko potters displayed their designs.

Because of an association with Korean pottery, Banko ware received little attention during the mid-1900s but has gained much popularity with collectors in the late-20th century. Examples from the late-1700s and early-1800s are rare but those from the later 19th century can still be found.

Japanese *Imari* is another style that evolved from Korean influence. It really refers to a group of porcelain producers named after the port town of Imari, possibly because this is where they were exported. In fact, Imari was so heavily exported with Dutch traders that it affected the Chinese export porcelain business.

Imari is often viewed as a porcelain decorated in an orange-red, dark blue and gold. Other recognizable styles of Imari that collectors should study include:

Sometsuke: Underglaze blue and white
Nishikide: A patterned polychrome
Gosai: Done in five colors
Sansai: Done in three colors

Other Imari is referred to by the name of the porcelain producing area or name of the company. The most common examples are Fukagawa Company, Hirado Island, Kakiemon (near Arita) and Nabeshima. Imari is still produced today and collectors need to study the differences between the old and new.

The iron Japanese teapots made from the late-1800s to the present, were manufactured in only a few places, especially in the Morioka area, and were originally intended for heating water like a kettle, not for brewing tea. I have seen these same cast iron pots with infusers, so at some point, they were made for tea.

Although the side handle is quite practical, Japanese teapots have more often been produced with a bail handle of bamboo, reed or some material wrapped in rattan. These types of handles are durable and prevent the heat of the teapot from burning the hand.

Japanese teapots have long been fashioned in

INDIA AND CEYLON TEA PAVILIONS

WORLD'S FAIR ST LOUIS 1904

INDIA

CEYLON

An advertising card from the St. Louis World's Fair in 1904 where India and Ceylon Tea was represented in two pavilions. This card was used two years later by a merchant in Cincinnati. Directions are also given to brew tea.

figural forms. Early designs were representative of the culture in shapes of animals, *Hotei* (or *Hirado*) man and his sack and/or *Hotei* with a child, fruit such as the peach and houses or other buildings. (Hirado and Hotei are the names of places.) Dragons have been produced more than any other figural. Banko ware teapots were often figural shapes of animals such as an elephant, bird, monkey, rabbit or duck.

European porcelain manufactures began copying the various figural forms of Japanese teapots only then the tide changed and the Japanese have been reproducing English-styled teapots from the latter part of the 19th century to the present. Many Japanese figural teapots are works of art with rich hand-painted detail and slip work such as Satsuma. Others are simple forms sold in quantity to retail establishments.

By the 20th century, novelty teapots found quite a following, as did imitations of more expensive European or English styles. Geisha Girl Porcelain is one pattern of highly exported Japanese ware and made by many potteries. Children's toy tea sets and souvenir teapots were produced in Geisha Girl. Reproductions of Geisha porcelain are still made today and sometimes can be found in import stores. Geisha porcelain portrays Japanese women in a wide variety of activities although the traditional Geisha was a woman trained in the arts and more particularly for entertainment.

Geisha porcelain was decorated with a trademark orange-red painted detail, although borders may be cobalt and other colors used within the scenes. Early pieces were all hand-painted and later ones done with a stencil or transfer printed outline and then hand-painted detail. Quite often the brush strokes are visible. Some pieces of Geisha are high-quality bone china and exquisitely hand-

decorated demanding very high prices. Others are medium to poor quality with sloppy detail and paint running into unwanted areas. Many styles and shapes of teapots, along with tea sets, were produced in the Geisha Girl porcelain. (See Reference Section for a book on Geisha Girl.)

One of the other fine porcelain or china productions coming from Japan is that of the Noritake Company. Producing ware from 1904 to the present, collectors should watch for the mark of an "M" in a wreath which actually indicates Noritake, distributed by the Morimura Brothers and was used until 1941. One of the most well-known patterns is that of Azalea, which was produced and distributed through the Larkin Company. This company, founded in 1875 by John Durant Larkin in Buffalo, N.Y., distributed soap and later many other household items. The Larkin offered an extensive premium listing of items available upon purchase of cases of soap or other toiletries. A 1915 ad shows a "Tea Ball Teapot" in the Noritake Azalea pattern. The description states that it

A postcard advertising Formosa Oolong tea, which was given free to patrons at the Lewis and Clark Centennial Exposition in Portland, Oregon, 1905.

was "Blue and white vitreous china" and this teapot features a built-in teaball hooked to a chain coming out of the lid. "...by chain attached, it can be withdrawn from water and secured in the cover as soon as infusion is of right strength. This assures a perfect cup of tea..." Price is listed at $1. Many patterns of Noritake china were offered through the Larkin, such as Sharon, Sheridan, Savoy, Briarcliff, Winthrop and Scenic. This company also distributed many other made-in-Japan teapots and tea sets as premiums.

Noritake is a finely crafted china with great attention to detailed decoration. Almost every pattern offered a teapot, sometimes changing the style or shape over the years. Gilt and gold decoration and those with hand-painted scenes are favorites among collectors but for ages it has been sold in fine china departments and the patterns are often chosen for bridal registries. Many patterns are currently in stock and collectors need to study vintage and modern Noritake before purchasing just because the name is familiar. There are good reference books on this subject.

During the 1950s, teapots made in Japan can be recognized by painted detail done over a glossy glaze. This paint chips off easily, especially when washed; examples with paint intact are more valuable. Wire bail handles were used for figural shapes of colonial people or majolica-styled pots with fruit and leaves in relief. Marks vary from an impressed or raised "Japan" or no mark at all. Paper labels began to be used extensively in the 1950s and were often removed. Teapots with a paper label have a higher value because of this fact.

One Japanese factory produced a majolica-style pottery which is a light, bisque-type clay and marked "Maruhan Ware." Collectors quickly snap up these pots because of their colorful detail and majolica styling. In the late-1950s and early-1960s, stacking sets were made in Japan in shapes like a black cat or deer. Some molds were even used to make similar animals with only the head being different—somehow the body fit for a rabbit, deer or cow!

Here are some guidelines for Japanese marks and when they were used:

Nippon: Means Japan and was used on various marks from 1891 to 1921. It is also the name of a Japanese ceramics factory and the word still appears in their markings.

Made in Japan: Used from 1921 into the 1960s. Some records state it was used until 1940, but many examples of porcelain and china teapots exist with "Made in Japan" which were produced after 1940.

Occupied Japan: Used after WWII, the years normally considered to be 1945 through 1952. Some accounts state that items with this mark did not reach American shores until 1948. Considering that much stock would have been already marked when the occupation ended, the date that occupied Japan items continued to be imported and sold could be extended also.

Japan and/or paper labels: These have been used from about 1953 to the present. Some items do not include the name Japan but can be recognized as being made in Japan. Examples of such marks include those from Lefton China and Enesco. When the only mark states "Hand-painted," it's very likely made in Japan.

Two of the modern names in ceramics distribution, especially for teapots, are the Otagiri Company and Fitz & Floyd. Both import whimsical and delightful figural teapots such as dancing bunnies or many Christmas designs. Otagiri actually makes ceramics and one of their previous designers left to form the business of Fitz & Floyd. Fitz & Floyd, on the other hand, is a marketing company which works to design ceramic items here in the United States but are produced in either Japan, Taiwan or Korea. Otagiri produces a lightweight, white porcelain which is prone to chipping but its figurals are enchanting with colorful details. The Fitz & Floyd company markets to higher end retail establishments with a finer porcelain product. Much attention is given to the hand-painted detail on any Fitz & Floyd teapot with prices often starting at about $70. for new items. Depending upon the piece, some secondary market prices have not risen to the same level.

There are many good reference sources which include teapots made in Japan (see Reference Section). The best way to collect these teapots successfully is to know the various types of decorations and the differences between pottery, porcelain or china. Teapots made in Japan have seen an increased collectibility in recent years which is sure to continue.

European Teapots

Tea and teapots were introduced to European countries from China, first exported to Holland and then to other countries. Chinese merchants in Holland refer to tea as ch'a, which is from an Amoy dialect. Tea steadily grew in popularity, along with Chinese export porcelain (including teapots and tea ware), which arrived in Holland, Germany and other European countries. By 1637, the Dutch East India Company was importing Chinese and Japanese tea with every ship because of the growing market. European potters envied the Chinese export porcelain and were trying to perfect a formula for the hard-paste body. In Holland, teapots were made with a tin-glazed soft-paste, but they invariably cracked under the stress of boiling water.

In the early 1700s, German chemist Johann Friedrich Bottger produced a teapot of a red-bodied porcelain, and had perfected the process by 1709. Founding the Meissen factory in 1710, porcelain teapots and dinnerware were first produced for the royal family. In several years, Meissen porcelain was sold on the open market.

With the discovery of porcelain, a method which eventually leaked out to other factories, teapots were fashioned after those imported from China. Studying examples now found in museums or books, European teapots from the 1700s portray an Oriental influence in style and decoration.

Much of the porcelain of this period in Italy, Spain and France was soft-paste. A worker from the Miessen factory was employed by the Vezzi factory in Italy, where he brought the secret porcelain formula. This was the third place in Europe to produce a hard-paste porcelain, only after Miessen and Vienna. There was a logistics problem because kaolin had to be shipped from Germany to produce porcelain. Other Italian porcelain producers included Cozzi, Doccia and more well-known to Americans, Capodimonte.

Capodimonte is a royal palace in Naples, Italy, and much of the early ware was produced for the court. Porcelain made from 1743-1759 at Capodimonte is considered some of the finest Italian ware. When the king of Naples became the king of Spain in 1759, the porcelain factory was moved near Madrid. Charles III took pride in his Capodimonte porcelain, moving the entire factory, equipment, workers and all. In 1834, the Doccia factory of Florence purchased the molds and has continued production. Porcelain and pottery are still produced with Capodimonte marks, and collectors need to study the marks used through the ages. Beautiful teapots and tea sets were made by all of the aforementioned manufacturers. Reproductions have been made by many companies in several countries.

Tea was introduced to France via a rival to the East India Company, called the *Compagnie des Indes*. At first, tea was considered more of an herbal medicine in France. *Veilleuses-theieres* (or night light teapots) were fashioned to aid in this infusion. The popularity of tea was growing in Britain, and the French people thought this was just because they had no wine in England. Being the fashion-conscious people the French are, taking tea was vogue during the late 1800s. In the late-20th century, taking tea at public establishments is once again the fashionable thing to do.

Pottery and porcelain manufacturers in France have produced wonderful teapots and tea sets. Examples from the 1700s are definitely decorated with an Oriental influence. Teapots were made by companies such as St. Cloud, Sevres, Chantilly and Tournai. Today, collectors are more apt to find teapots made by French factories such as Haviland and other Limoge companies.

The Haviland company has a long and interesting history dating back to 1842. An American china importer, David Haviland, moved to Limoges, France, where china was specifically made for the American market. Haviland has produced thousands of patterns of china in the last 100 years. To aid in decorating its china, Haviland pioneered the decal decorating process. One of Haviland's sons, Theodore, opened an American factory in 1936 which still operates today. Collectors should refer to one of the many books on Haviland to study marks and patterns. Innumerable teapots have been made by Haviland and the majority are part of a dinnerware line.

English Teapots

In 1649, England's royal family exiles to Holland after Cromwell takes over and Charles I was beheaded. Tea was fashionable in Holland at the time when the little prince and future king (Charles II) was growing up. By 1658, tea had recently been introduced to England where it was sold in coffee houses. It was a controversial drink. Some thought it to be a virtual cure-all and others proclaimed that it was evil. In 1664, the British Commonwealth is restored with a king whose favorite drink is tea. Queen Catherine was from Portugal, where she was raised on tea. Together, Charles and Catherine were the first British Royalty to drink tea.

Chinese teapots were imported to England along with the crates of tea. The wealthy and aristocracy embraced the drinking of tea, and potteries were producing a wide variety of teapots. During the Georgian period, tea drinking was associated with a stylish and refined way of life. Tea time offered a way to exhibit wealth and elaborately decorated pottery and porcelain were an important part of taking tea.

Silver teapots were formed and the earliest known pot was presented to the East India Company in 1670. The more well-to-do would commission the local silversmith to make their silver teapot.

Pieces were added as desired or needed, often as special occasion gifts and inscribed with names, dates or family initials.

Josiah Wedgwood of the long-standing Wedgwood company had his beginnings with partner Thomas Wheildon. In 1759, Wedgwood established his own pottery where he continually invented new types of porcelain and the jasperware that Wedgwood is quite famous for. Wheildon continued to produced pottery, hiring and training Josiah Spode. In 1770, Spode began his own pottery, producing the transfer-printed blue-and-white patterns for which they are still famous. Spode is credited with inventing bone china in 1800. This company partnered with William Taylor Copeland in 1833 and has seen many changes through the years. A favorite with collectors is the Spode's "Tower" pattern which is a Willow variant. White china and porcelain decorated in blue patterns is still produced by the company today by a descendant of William Tay-

Pink roses decorate this modern teapot by Crown Dorset. Markings are: crown, "Fine Bone China, Staffordshire Fine Ceramics, England." This set is beautiful, while being durable enough for every day tea or special guests. This set has a $75 value.

lor Copeland. Teapots in the traditional London shape are especially desirable.

The Staffordshire area has been home to many potteries in the last two centuries, which produced teapots along with other items. Today, collectors scour the Stoke-on-Trent area outside of London, which the name given to several town. The many pottery, porcelain and china companies have located their factory stores in this area. This area is so popular that a special bus ticket can be purchased called a "China Day Rider," allowing visitors all day on and off privileges for shopping this area.

Other areas of England have also offered up their teapots for practical use and collectible purposes through the years. Burslem, England, is frequently found along with the backstamp on a teapot. Bristol and Plymouth are where potteries have been established. One of the wonderful things about all of the teapots made in England over the last three centuries is that many of the same companies are still doing business. Antiques and collectibles reference books have information on many of these companies, and Internet websites are available on others.

American Teapots

Soon after tea and teapots were being produced in England, they came across the sea to the New World. The East India Trading Company was growing during the late-1700s and was shipping tea and Chinese porcelain to the New England.

Very little porcelain and pottery was produced in America before the 1800s. One of the earliest recorded companies is that of William Ellis Tucker of Philadephia. Most pieces were unmarked. Other potteries manufactured salt-glazed stoneware with New York and New Jersey being a good source for stoneware clay.

One of the most famous pottery areas is Bennington, Vt. The United States Pottery Company of Bennington established the production of Rockingham-style pottery in America. This mottled brown glaze pottery was made by many potteries in New Jersey, Pennsylvania, Maryland, Massachusetts, New York and Ohio. The Norton-Fenton partnership in Bennington also produced teapots in the Rockingham style.

Edwin Bennett, an English potter, opened his

Pink and gray lustre swirls on this teapot are referred to as Surf Ballet, made by California artist Sasha Brastoff. The mark includes the artist name and chanticleer (rooster) used since 1953. This especially large items sells for $250.

pottery in Baltimore in 1846. This is one of the many potteries to produce the Rebekah at the Well teapot. It was also during the 1840s that clay beds in the Ohio River valley were discovered. East Liverpool and Zanesville, Ohio, have been pottery and porcelain production centers ever since.

Most of the potteries of the Ohio River Valley began in the late-1800s or early-1900s. Some of the well-known companies in the Ohio River valley include Rookwood, Weller, Hall China, Homer Laughlin, Nelson McCoy, McCoy, Limoge China, Wheeling, Shawnee, Pope-Gosser, Knowles Taylor Knowles and Edwin M. Knowles. There have been other potteries in this area, and almost all have produced teapots. Some of them are still in production today, while others closed up after World War II.

American pottery and porcelain companies have received much attention in the last 30 years of the 20th century. Once overlooked for imported ware, teapots made in America have been the subject of much research and many books. This focus has caused heightened collectibility with prices rising and teapots sought after.

Clay beds were also discovered in the Los Angeles Basin of California; during the first half of the 20th century, many potteries sprang up in this area. Ware from the California potteries has seen a surge in the last decade. Most of these companies produced highly decorated teapots, some times as part of a dinnerware line.

Names to watch for include Sasha Brastoff, Franciscan, Metlox, Vernon Kilns and Winfield. See the Resources Section for reference books.

Collectors would do well to purchase teapots made in the United States whenever possible as long as the price is within reason. The value will surely increase and the character of these teapots will add to your collection.

Advertising card for the Boston and Springfield Tea Co. There's no indication of the city where this tea company was located. Lithograph appears to be from early-1900s.

Places of Interest

Teapot Exhibits, Displays and Events

What could be more fun than finding teapots for your own collection? Visiting other collections, of course. Many art galleries and museums schedule regular teapot themed events or exhibits. Should you visit any public display of teapots, sign the guest book or get on the mailing list so you'll know when the next similar event is held.

A new gallery in Los Angeles has opened dedicated to teapots: Parham Gallery of Fine and Exotic Teapots. Like many galleries, the teapots are artistic renditions, not something ready to brew your favorite tea. One of these teapots could be your next tea time conversation piece. Although most galleries have a selection that can honestly be used for tea, most teapots are meant to tickle your fancy rather than tempt your taste buds. At Parham Gallery, owner John Parham exudes his excitement for modern artists and their imaginative, original interpretations of the teapot.

In total dedication to the enjoyment of teapots, one whole town is known for teapots: Trenton, Tenn. Not only do the residents boast an Annual Teapot Festival, but they proudly display the world's largest collection of Porcelain Veilleuse-Theieres—night-light teapots. This permanent exhibit of 525 teapots was donated by Dr. Frederick C. Freed to his hometown and is displayed in the city Municipal Building. These Veilleuses-Theieres are large with ornate and exquisite stands, first made about 1830 in France. This collection represents more than 18 countries where they've been manufactured. Many are figural people and animals, with a base for a candle or oil hidden inside. Others are works of art in porcelain such as the Limoges, France Gothic cathedral design c1830. Not only can this beatiful collection be viewed, but, for two weeks in May every year, an assortment of teapot-themed activities are held in Trenton, including a parade, teapot rope pull, a teapot trot (dance) and a hometown hospitali-tea. (See reference section for contact details.)

Another collection of Veilleuse-Theieres is at the Wadsworth Antheneum in Hartford, Conn. On display are 177 teapot night lights from the Harold and Wendy Newman Collection.

Other less pretentious exhibits can be viewed in the United States, England and even China. The China National Tea Museum is located in Hangzhou, China, where exhibits display the history of tea, tea produced in China, teapots and tea utensils.

Mills College in Oakland, Calif., is home to sev-

eral hundred teapots collected by Susan Tolman Mills, wife of the college founder. The collection is now preserved by the Alumni Association.

In London, the Victoria and Albert Museum has an extensive teapot exhibit. Some of the oldest existing teapots can be viewed at this London museum. Many teapots from the Victoria and Albert collection have been featured in magazine articles and books. The museum has a gift shop where you might find replica teapots from their collection.

The Twining Teapot Gallery is home to 2,600 teapots from two private collections, with a majority dating from the 18th century. The Gallery is located in Norwich Castle, about 80 miles north of London. The oldest part of this collection was acquired in 1946 at the bequest of Colonel E.A. Bulwer of Heydon Grange, Norfolk, a great connoisseur in his day. Another part of the collection was acquired in 1988 and was the private collection of Philip Miller, author and teapot expert. Twinings saved Miller's extensive collection from dispersal, knowing that a great deal of history would be lost if the collection was broken up. The Twining Teapot Gallery is considered the greatest collection of British teapots in the world.

In Toronto, visitors to the George R. Gardiner Museum of Ceramic Art will find a limited number

of teapots, but examples well worth the trip. The Museum is dedicated to pottery and porcelain with exhibits of Pre-Columbian Pottery, Italian Maiolica and English Delftware. The second floor is dedicated to porcelain where an exquisite Meissen cup and saucer and a Worcester teapot can be viewed, both from the 1700s.

If you can't travel to wonderful museums, galleries and collections, you can still view other teapots from your own home if you have Internet access. The sites which have teapots for sale, teapot history, tea and every type of accoutrement are far more than can be listed in this book. If you don't want to spend a lot of time searching various web sites, then go directly to any of the sampling listed in the Reference Section. Many of the places I've listed have color images of beautiful teapots.

Always be sure to call or write museums or galleries to verify days and hours they are open along with entrance fees. Remember that exhibits or museums not specific to teapots may have one or two on display and are well worth the visit. While visiting a maritime musuem, several teapots were located throughout the ship—not something you'd expect.

Take some time to see other collections because no one museum or collector can have all the teapots.

THE TEAPOTS

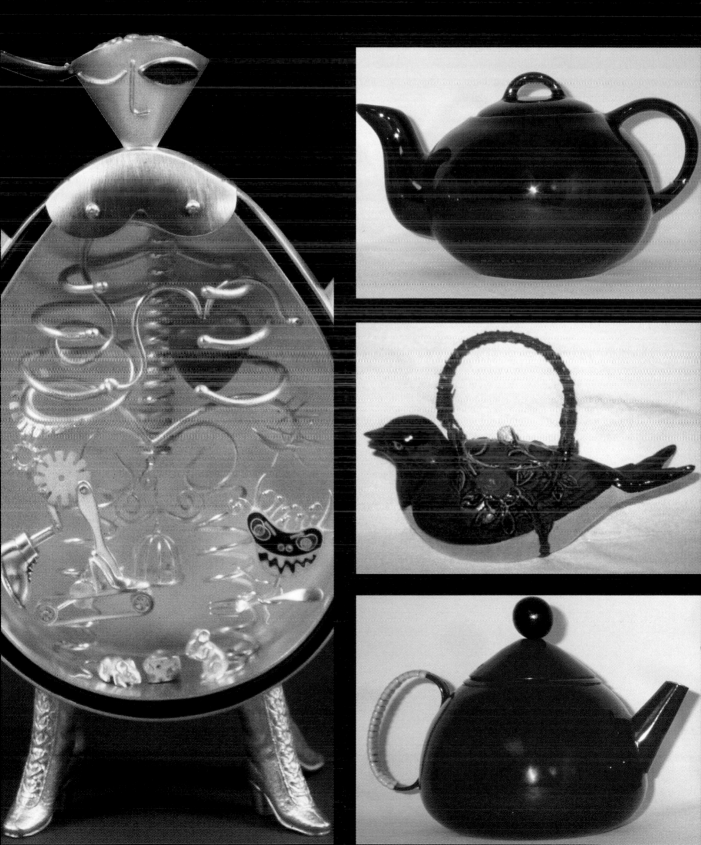

This section of the book is broken into 16 different categories or styles of teapots. A description of that type of teapot will be given, some historical background and names of companies that produced those teapots. Other useful information such as reproduction alerts and what collectors are finding in that category will be given if available. Then you will find a price guide listing of teapots for that category which includes teapots not illustrated here. All teapots shown in the photos will have a description and approximate value.

When using the price guide values, remember that these represent teapots in mint or excellent condition. That is to say they have no chips, flaws or damage. Prices for teapots with some wear or flaws should be reduced to reflect their condition. Prices reflect market value. This is the price you would see on that particular teapot in an antique store or other retail establishment. Remember that a teapot is worth what someone is willing to pay. Use these figures as a gauge to give you an idea of what your teapot is worth. Collectors purchase teapots from sources which run the whole spectrum of prices. Auction houses, antique shops, flea markets, swap meets, yard or rummage sales, gift shops and tea shops have unique methods of pricing. Some are based on a percentage of wholesale, others are just good guesses which provide a happy margin of profit. All of the above affect the price of a teapot which may differ greatly from those listed in this book.

Antiques and collectibles prices also greatly differ depending upon the area of the United States in which it is being offered. Sources on the East Coast and West Coast states generally have higher prices than middle states and some southern areas.

Remember that sentimental value knows no price. If your teapot means more than any price tag, keep it or give it to someone who will appreciate and care for it.

Front left: Lipton premium by Fraunfelter, mark is "Lipton's Tea" ($40); front right: Lipton premium by Hall China in the French shape, mark is "Lipton's Tea" ($45); and back: Lipton premium creamer and sugar, Boston shape, mark is "Lipton's Tea" ($40 for set).

Advertising, Souvenir & Commemorative Teapots

dvertising, souvenir and commemorative teapots are actually three categories related by the fact that the decoration on these teapots represents people, places, a company or a special date in history. These categories are listed according to their original and current secondary market values with advertising being the lowest, souvenirs at the mid-range level and commemoratives commanding the highest values.

Advertising Teapots

Advertising teapots promote a product or company in hopes that sales will be generated. Other teapots with advertising on them were premium items which could be obtained after purchasing a product. The teapot might have been offered for some proof of purchase or may have also required an additional cost.

The Hall China Company of East Liverpool, OH, has produced premium offer teapots since the 1930s for other companies. Two of its most

McCormick teapots, made by Hall China, both have a strainer that sits inside the teapot opening, only a white rim of the strainers is showing. Mark on these teapots is impressed on the bottom and reads "McCormick & Co. Banquet Teas, Balto," late-1930s to 1940s. Turquoise teapot ($50), brown with gold ($75).

Brown glazed teapot made by Royal Caldone, Ceracraft, England and marked on the bottom, for "Mrs. Bridges, Original Country Kitchen, for a Perfect Cup of Tea" ($65); brown coralene decoration on this advertising teapot for Tokay Tea, impressed PBB, England mark, possibly Price Brothers ($75). (from the collection of Suze Richmond, Missouri)

well-known were for McCormick Tea and Lipton Tea, although Hall China has produced teapots for many other companies.

One of the highly collected Hall China premium items began in 1933, called Autumn Leaf for the Jewel Tea Company. A teapot was produced in 1933 in its Newport shape and discontinued in 1935 then reissued in the 1970s. Other Autumn Leaf decorated teapots were made through the years including the Aladdin shape in 1942 and offered until 1976. Hall China ceased Autumn Leaf-pattern production in 1978. But this pattern has won the hearts of many a collector to the degree that in 1990, China Specialties, Inc., commissioned Hall China to produce Autumn Leaf teapots. It began with the airflow shape, but in the last decade, China Specialties has marketed many Hall China Autumn Leaf teapots including the Aladdin and the Automobile. (See Resources Section for contact information.)

The Hall name was included on some items, but not all, causing some confusion among collec-tors. Hall's motto, Superior Quality, was used on many items produced for other companies, which can aid collectors in identifying those without the "Hall" mark.

For the obvious reason of selling tea, the most common advertising on a teapot has been for tea distributors. Salada, Tokay, McCormick, Lipton, Ming, Tetley, Tipperar and Ty-Phoo tea compa-nies have all been represented on a teapot. Many organizations have also commissioned teapots as fund-raisers, gifts or limited editions. Examples are the Jim Beam Bottle Collector's Club, Har-rods, Ltd. of London, KitKat, Mrs. Bridges Country Kitchen and even The Art Institute of Chicago's Frank Lloyd Wright Exhibit. While most advertising teapots were made since 1950, their value lies in the fact that most were pro-duced in limited quantities.

A different twist on advertising was used when a teapot was marketed to support World War II efforts. (See the Pottery Section for more details on this teapot made in England.)

McCormick Tea House, fashioned to represent its Baltimore site, c1980s ($40). (photo courtesy of Gary Stotsky, Pennsylvania)

Souvenir Teapots

The appeal of souvenir teapots is directly related to the association with a place, especially home-towns, childhood memories or vacations. Souvenir teapots may represent a town, capitol building, a tourist attraction or theme park. The earliest souvenir items were produced in the Staffordshire area of London in the 1820s through the 1850s, with transfer-printed designs often depicting the expanding United States.

Once you start collecting souvenir teapots, you'll begin to differentiate between modern decals, designs of the 1950s or transfer painted scenes of the 1930s and 1940s. Cobalt blue glazes were popular in the late-1800s and early-1900s and predominantly made in Germany. Examples include a lot of gold trim.

There were several American distributors of pictorial or souvenir china; while their names may be on the backstamp, they were not the original manufacturer. One of the largest of these companies was CE Wheelock & Co., out of Peoria, IL, and South Bend, IN. This firm distributed all across the United States from 1888-1971, but its souvenir items, such as teapots, are most plentiful in the Ohio Valley.

John H. Roth, one of the officers of the Wheelock company, formed his own business in 1909 and souvenirs will bear his mark of "JonRoth" and the name of the merchant for which the items were produced. This pictorial china came from Germany and England; after 1940, it was only from England with a mark of "Old English Staffordshire Ware."

For collectors of Wedgwood, the Jones, McDuffee & Stratton company distributed items made by Wedgwood from about 1880 through the 1940s.

The value of souvenir teapots is determined by the popularity of the location and methods of decoration. Cobalt blue examples are sought after by collectors, along with those with transfer designs and hand-painted detail. Souvenir items also tend to become more valuable the closer they are to the point of representation. The value of a Florida teapot will be highest in that state. Some souvenir teapot collectors watch for those representing each of the 50 states, no matter where they are located. Souvenir teapots become a crossover collectible when they are a commemorative, dated for a special event. There are a couple of good books on souvenir china to help research these teapots.

Top: Marineland of the Pacific, white metal S&Ps, red plastic finial, Japan mark ($18); bottom: Tycer Pottery, Zanesville, Ohio, pottery with maroon glaze, no mark, U.S.A. ($25).

From left: Little America, 3-piece set, Wyoming, heavy gold trim, no mark, remnants of label ($22); Santa's Village, 3-piece set, Dundee, IL, paper label, Japan, c1960 ($18); I Love Grandma, 3-piece set, Giftique label, Toronto, made in Japan ($18).

From left: Cobalt, Lewis and Clark Expo, Portland, OR, no mark, Germany ($40); Owen Sound Harbour, no mark, applied gold decoration, two-tone, possibly Germany ($35); cobalt, tall pot with scene of Queenstown, made in Germany mark, gold trim ($45).

San Francisco, 3 pc. set, hand-painted and heavy gold trim, no mk., Japanese ($22); Oklahoma, 3-pc. set, Indian chief & oil rigs, no mk., Japanese ($18); California Redwoods, hand-painted over-all design, label Victoria Ceramics Japan ($22).

From left: Washington, DC, transfer and hand-painted, made in Germany mark, gold trim ($40); Pikes Peak, CO, miniature sized souvenir, Japan mark, bone china, decal and hand-painted ($18); Cliffs Near Newport Beach, transfer design, made in Germany mark, gold trim ($35).

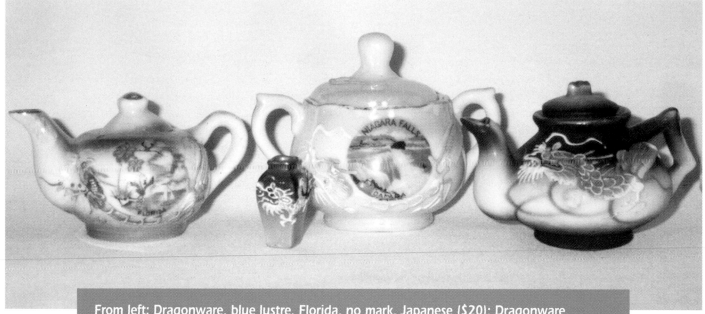

From left: Dragonware, blue lustre, Florida, no mark, Japanese ($20); Dragonware, miniature vase, marked Japan ($15); Dragonware, covered sugar, Niagara Falls, mark, made in Japan ($18); Dragonware, black and gray, no mark, Japanese ($20).

From left: hand-painted detail, Mackinac Bridge, Michigan souvenir set, paper sticker states, "A Quality Product, Made in Japan" ($20); individual sized Michigan souvenir teapot from 1950s, state animal, the Beaver, is finial and handle, backstamp made in Japan ($25).

Commemorative Teapots

Commemorative teapots are made to celebrate and mark a special occasion or people. The majority have been for United Kingdom royalty, and collectors today are focusing on those of Princess Diana. The wonderful thing about commemorative teapots is that the majority will have dates on them, eliminating any search for age. Even those without dates can often be determined with a bit of historical fact finding (know when Queen Victoria reigned and you'll know the time period of a teapot with her picture). In this case, further commemorative details may be needed because Queen Victoria reigned from 1837-1901. Long live the Queen.

Commemorative teapots and other items have become highly collectible in the late-20th century. Not only have they been made in pottery or porcelain, but aluminum has also been used. The Swan Brand Tea Company produced a teapot commemorating the Coronation of Elizabeth II in 1953. Another aluminum individual-sized teapot was made to celebrate the Festival of Britain in the 1950s. A reference book is available, along with a newsletter giving current values and availability of commemorative items. (See Reference Section for details.)

Trends for advertising, souvenir and commemorative teapots will include any advertising which has been commonplace and overlooked such as the small Ming Tea Co. teapots; souvenir items from the 1950s and 1960s will increase in desirability with the new millennium; commemorative teapots of Princess Diana and those celebrating America's bicentennial will be sought after. Collectors should continue to watch for teapots made in England and the United States in all of the above categories, while those made in other countries will increase in value because of their availability.

Commemorative teapots of Charles and Diana. At left: small teapot of brown pottery, impressed design on the side with 1981 date and names, mark is impressed "CM, Wales" ($95); white china with decal of the Royal Couple, description on back, "Their Royal Highnesses, The Prince and Princess of Wales," no mark on bottom, English or German blank used ($110).

SOUVENIR TEAPOTS

The appeal of souvenir teapots is associated with a place either somewhere you've visited, from a hometown or even a childhood memory. Souvenir china or porcelain is often referred to as pictorial china and these teapots can quickly become one of your "collections within a collection."

During the Industrial Revolution, vacationing and tourism reached new heights. Out of this grew the demand for souvenirs. Souvenir teapots are pieces of history depicting the styles, activities, architecture and landscape of a particular era. As scenery, buildings and fashions changed, it was preserved on this cheerful porcelain.

Avid souvenir collectors hunt for examples popular during the late-1800s and early-1900s, made in Germany with cobalt glazes. Pictorial souvenir china made in Germany and England was distributed by many American companies, which often included their names and the name of the merchant selling the end product. Some of the more well-known distributors were are CE Wheelock & Co.; John H. Roth & Co.; Jones, McDuffee & Stratton, Co.; Rowland & Marsellus; A.C. Bosselman & Co.; George H. Bowman Co.; and Wright, Tyndale and van Roden.

In the 1930s, souvenir teapots were made by U.S. companies. By the 1940s, pictorial china was exported from Japan. These items were predominantly decorated with decal souvenir scenes and lettering either over the glaze or sometimes under a clear glaze. After World War II, souvenir teapots were produced in large quantities in Japan—the most common being a three-piece set including a small teapot, a cup and a saucer on a stand. To determine age, check the stands: Older ones are made from wood, newer ones from plastic. Souvenir tea sets from the last 20 years use thick enamel paint for decoration and multi-colored designs with modern type-styles. In the 1950s, majolica-style souvenir ware was made in Japan where Items representative of the place were molded in relief. For example: an Indian chief and beavers or state names.

Collecting souvenir items, particularly teapots and tea sets, has grown in popularity since the 1980s when a collectors' association was formed. Available now are a couple reference guides along with sections in many antique and collectible price guides. Souvenir teapots don't command the higher prices of fine china and prices range from $15 for a small set made in Japan to $75 for a cobalt pot made in Germany. Medium-sized china teapots, such as a souvenir of the Morrison Hotel in Chicago, are valued between $28-$35.

Souvenir teapots are readily available and generally inexpensive enough to allow new collectors a place to begin. The next time you visit a theme park, truck stop or well-known tourist attraction, check for teapots in their souvenir sections and you may add a teapot that serves as a reminder of your visit.

From left: "Brew Up" Savings bank is made of ceramic and coated to look like metal, souvenir of Main Street Market House but location is unknown, no mark, Japan ($15); restaurant ware marked "Cooks Hotel & Restaurant Supply, New York, Jackson China" ($35).

Bottom of "Cooks" restaurant teapot, mark is ink backstamp under clear glaze, note that the lid has deep under rim to help prevent slipping off when being poured.

Salt and pepper souvenirs, all made in Japan (from left): aerial view of Niagra Falls, c1950s ($25); Disneyland, c1980s ($18); souvenir of Fort Randall Dam c1950s ($25).

Two toy-sized souvenir tea sets, from left: Bear Creek Scenic Railroad, North Carolina, china, marked "Japan" in red, c1950s ($25); Mt. Rushmore National Monument, Black Hills, South Dakota, china, marked "Japan" in red, with cups and saucers, c1960s ($25).

Two toy-sized souvenir tea sets, from left; Queen Mary, china, hand-painted detail, marked "Made in Japan," c1960s ($25); Catholic Shrine, Indian River, Michigan, teapot missing, note detail on saucer, c1960s ($20).

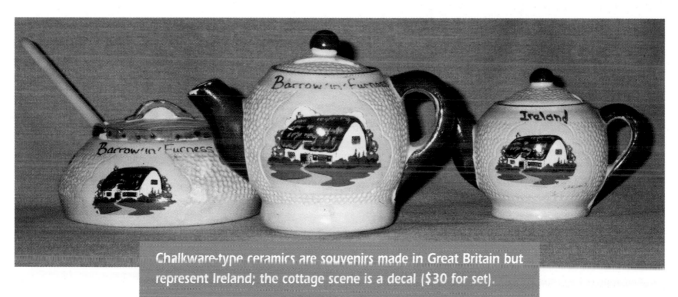

Chalkware-type ceramics are souvenirs made in Great Britain but represent Ireland; the cottage scene is a decal ($30 for set).

Salt & pepper souvenirs; all made in Japan (from left): Florida, hand-painted ocean scene, marked "Made in Japan," c1940s-1950s ($22); Castle Rock, St. Ignace, Mich., marked "Japan," c1930s-1940s ($25); The Ozarks, paper sticker "Japan," hand-painted over transfer, c1950s ($18).

From left: Maryland, individual-sized pot, flag symbol, white porcelain, no mark ($15), commemorative pot of Gettysburg, PA, impressed Canada mark, c1960s ($38); Bonomelli Nice Tea, white porcelain, individual-sized pot, ACF Porzellan mark ($15).

McCormick teapot in a common lettuce green and white with silver detail, mark reads "McCormick & Co., Banquet Teas, Balto," c1940s ($50).

Made in Russia, square-shaped pot commemorates Moscow Olympics, modern ($85). (photo courtesy of Gary Stotsky, Pennsylvania)

Top and bottom left: 1650 tea set designates the establishment of Davison Newman & Co., Ltd., mark on bottom for same and "Boston Tea Parties, 1773-1774," to commemorate event, c1973-1974 ($95 for set); bottom right: George Washington, Martha on opposite side, no mark, possibly U.S., same decals used by many companies, Bicentennial of Washington's birthday, celebrated 1932 ($55).

Advertising, Souvenir & Commemorative Teapots

ITEM	VALUE
1776-1976, blue and white porcelain, 6-cup size, made in England	$45.00
Bear Creek Scenic Railroad, toy set, Japan, 3 pieces with lids	$15.00
Charles & Diana, toy set including the two little princes, 7-pieces with lids, white china, England	$100.00
Edward VII, 1901-1909, pink lustre and gold, England	$300.00
Franklin Mint, set of six, The Great Tea Merchants, each pot a tea company	$200.00
George VI, 1937 Coronation, 2-cup, by Gibsons, England, some Art Deco styling	$185.00
Ireland, chalkware-type pottery, cottage design for many places, England, c1960	$20.00
John Wesley, reproduction issued in 1950s, marked Wedgwood, England	$95.00
London Bridge, Lake Havasu City, AZ, modern, paper label, Japan, 3 pieces	$20.00
Masons, small, white porcelain pot with Eastern star decal, Japan, Enesco	$50.00
New York World's Fair, 1940, Hall China, star shape, gold decoration	$450.00
New York World's Fair, 1940, off-white porcelain, earthtone decor, Porcelier, USA	$100.00
Old Faithful Geyser, Yellowstone, JonRoth mark, made by Royal Winton, England	$95.00
Puerto Rico, cobalt and gold, Japan, c1970	$12.00
Queen Elizabeth II, 1953 Coronation, gold lustre teapot, wheat decor, Sadler, England	$130.00
Queen Mary, toy set, 7 pieces, Japan, applied decal of ship	$22.00
Queen Mother's 90th Birthday, 1990, 2-cup, white china with transfer of Queen, England	$80.00
Red Coach, Hall China Co., hotel/restaurant ware, c1970	$25.00
South Bend Indiana, gold overlay, marked Japan, 2 in.	$15.00
St. Anthony's Lighthouse, Falmouth, England, crown mark, china, 4-1/4-in. high	$50.00
Tea Company, advertising, reproduction, Oriental manufacture, c1990	$28.00
Tetley Tea, white porcelain, figure on lid, modern, by Lyons-Tetley Co.	$75.00
Tipperary Tea, large pot for window display, England, c1930	$95.00

Children's and Toy Teapots & Tea Sets

Teapots and tea sets made for little fingers are classified into the two highly collected categories of children's and toy items. Children's teapots or tea sets were made for children to actually use like an adult, possibly in their nursery. Toy teapots and tea sets were made for playing and pretending although some may actually hold liquid, the steeping of tea or spooning of sugar would be nearly impossible.

Children's Teapots and Tea Sets

Children's china and porcelain was made as early as 1750, but didn't come into widespread popularity until the 1800s, especially during the Victorian era. One of the perplexities of children's tea sets is that there was no standard for the number of pieces to a set, leaving collectors to determine whether or not a set is complete. A tea set could be as simple as a teapot, sugar, creamer and four cups, saucers and plates or containing a complex number of pieces including soup tureens, covered casseroles and platters.

Children's teapots or tea sets were intended for actual use and it's unusual to find them without the signs of wear such as chips and cracks. Even sets never used and still in their original boxes are rarely perfect because of damage from moving over the years. Collectors must accept the imperfections of teapots or tea sets and realize that little fingers were just learning how to care for breakable things. If you can imagine a gleeful tea party of girls, boys, bears and dolls, clinking the china as they sip their tea, munch the sandwiches and cake and giggling all the while, then your imperfect tea set will have a special charm all of its own.

Children's teapots from the 1800s are becoming harder to find but those from the 20th century are still available. Most decorated china or porcelain was made in England and Germany in the 19th

Tin tea set, Ohio Art Co., tray with 22 pieces, Blue Willow, c1950 ($125). The doll, So-Wee, is from the same era, made by Sun Rubber Co. ($150).

From left: Porcelain, decal of skating money with candy, marked "Edwin M. Knowles, U.S.A." ($30); Wedgwood, baby blue set of teapot, creamer and sugar and sugar like a small bowl, England, c1930 ($100).

From left: White bone china, gold trim with wear, no mark, German style ($30); Germany, Schlegelmilch, bone china, floral pattern, unique screw-on lid, c1930 ($45); Blue Willow, the teapot part of set, "Made in Occupied Japan" ($45).

From left: Victorian children playing, heavy china, no mark, Germany ($45); teapot, creamer and sugar, porcelain, marked "Germany" in double circle, c1930 ($75).

century; by the turn of the 20th century, American pottery companies were producing these small versions of their larger wares. By the 1940s, children's sets were made with nursery rhymes, popular cartoons or artist's designs such as Kate Greenaway.

Glass tea sets were produced by several American glass companies beginning in the 1930s, but gained popularity during World War II when imports were not as plentiful. The Akro Agate Company was the most popular maker (its glass teapots didn't have spouts but were more like pitchers). Other glass companies include the Hazel Atlas Co., Jeanette Glass Co., and the McKee Glass Co. Finding one of these sets in the original box is considered a special find by collectors.

Tea sets for use like adults became less popular by the late-1950s, but those intended for play continued to be made although the choice of materials changed from fine china to tin and plastic. The Ohio Art Co., made many tin tea sets in the 1950s and early-1960s. While these sets were marketed like toys, they were made for actual use, and some had extra pieces like a covered cake plate or tiny dessert plates. The J. Chein Co., and the Wolverine Co., made several styles of tin tea sets. During this same era, the Ideal Co., produced a wonderful plastic tea set modeled after the adult Russell Wright design called American Modern. The largest set was originally sold for $2.98.

Complicating the matter of collecting tea sets from the 1940s-1960s is the fact that different sized sets of the same pattern were marketed. Larger sets contained many extra pieces, while the basic set could be bought with just a teapot, creamer, sugar and two cups and saucers. In the 1960s, tea sets were made of aluminum and one company advertised a 29-piece set or a 31-piece set for $1 each (the difference was a choice of a drip coffee maker or a teapot).

A demitasse tea set is sometimes considered to be a children's set, although this was not the original intent. Actually, demitasse is a French word used for a small cup of strong coffee, and it's also the name given to these small cups. The cups of some tea sets were made in a smaller size and are referred to as demitasse possibly because of their similarity to the quaint coffee cups. Tea sets considered to be demitasse mimic the perfect size for children's use and were made from the 1960s to the present.

Today, children's tea sets are still produced but nothing can replace the china and porcelain from the turn of the 20th century, decorated with Victorian children or an array of animals. New sets can be purchased through mail order catalogs such as Horchow, The Smithsonian or The Country House (where two replica versions of tin sets are available). In the American Girl series, Molly celebrates her birthday with a tea party and the porcelain set is a reproduction of a similar 1940s style. The Godinger Silver Company (silverplate) has reproduced many tea-related items including a set on a tray in just the perfect size for children.

A modern picnic tea set, sure to lure any collector, has been offered by Lillian Vernon and in some larger department stores. Made in China, the portable 16-piece set fits snugly into a padded basket. The picnic tea set is decorated with blue flowers, made of a durable porcelain and imitates adult-sized traveling tea sets.

During the mid-1990s, 23-piece porcelain tea sets were marketed through large retailers and distributed by either PCCW Inc., or Murcures & Associates. Different themes were designs such as country farm, teddy bears, bunnies or circus time. These tea sets are children's sized and easily used for real tea and food. Besides the traditional teapot, creamer, sugar, cups and saucers, the set has extras like napkin rings and a platter. Each piece is molded in relief with the characters of the theme. The porcelain is light and easily chipped. Pieces have been showing up in antique stores with prices higher than a realized value. The problem is that marking on most pieces is a sticker "made in China" which easily comes off with washing. The cost for these sets new was $20; today complete sets in a box would be valued at $40.

Toy Teapots and Tea Sets

Toy teapots and tea sets have been produced in a variety of shapes, sizes and materials. They were intended for play and pretend and therefore don't have some of the functional features of children's tea sets, i.e. spouts aren't hollow, lids may be permanently attached. Toy teapots are some of the most charming and collectors search for those sets still in original boxes. They were meant to be used in play and it's difficult to find sets or pieces without some chips, wear in the design or missing lids.

Toy teapots or sets were fashioned after popular

Bear's tea time, 23 pieces, teapot mark 1996, gold label, made in China ($35).

Farm set, 23 pieces, teapot marked "Mercuries," 1994, paper label with same and made in China ($35 for set).

From left: China, gold decoration with wear, oblong shape, possibly part of a set, no mark, Germany ($40); white china, gold decoration, marked with letters, possibly part of a set, Germany ($35); white china, gold decoration, no mark, possibly part of a set, Germany ($40).

dolls, other toys and cartoon characters. Collectors are starting to snap up plastic sets made from the 1950s through the 1970s because these same themes are popular collectibles. Subjects such as Mickey & Minnie Mouse, Holly Hobbie, Barbie and Dolly Dingle are highly desirable. Fisher Price produced a heavy plastic "My First Tea Set" which is durable and appealing in a soft pink and white. Play-Doh made a "Tea for Two" set where tea time food could be molded from the pieces of the set. Even the teapot opened to reveal molds for a tea bag, sugar cubes and lemon slices.

Mail-order catalogs offer toy teapots or tea sets such as the pink porcelain set mimicking Wedgwood jasperware from "A Special Place" catalog. The Betty Crocker premium catalog has offered toy tea sets including one made in Germany and decorated with scenes of children playing.

Most toy teapots and sets were produced in Japan, and collectors watch for those marked "made in occupied Japan" although many other delicate sets were produced. A popular theme for toy teapots along with any other size is Blue Willow. This design has charmed children and adults for ages and toy-sized tea sets were made from the 1940s through the present, although today's examples are not always of the same high quality.

Collectors should watch for complete plastic sets and those from the 1950s and 1960s. Teapots or sets made since that time are growing in collectibility and those with popular themes will increase in value.

Picnic tea time, modern set in a basket, blue and white porcelain, Taiwan ($30). The handmade bear is made from Laura Ashley fabric and was made by Tania Brown from Michigan ($50).

This silverplated tea set is ready for company with two pots—one for tea and one for water—just like traditional silver tea sets. This set is by Paul Revere Silversmiths, distributed by Godinger Silver, New York, made in China ($35).

Toy tea sets from the early 20th century. From left: boxed set of bisque porcelain, two cups and saucers, not sugar, note the lithographic detail on the box lid, pieces not marked but box states "Made in Germany" ($65); set with mug-style cups, wear on the gold and flowers, pieces not marked, looks German ($45).

Toy tea set, lustre glaze, hand-painted decoration, with two cups and saucers, early 1950s ($35).

From left: Gold glazed tea sets on trays; no mark, thought to be made in England, late 1800s ($45); round shaped pot, no mark, possibly Germany or Japan, c1930 ($35).

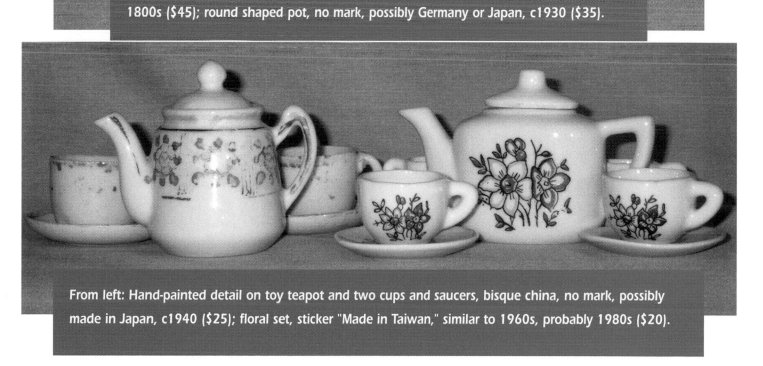

From left: Hand-painted detail on toy teapot and two cups and saucers, bisque china, no mark, possibly made in Japan, c1940 ($25); floral set, sticker "Made in Taiwan," similar to 1960s, probably 1980s ($20).

Two boxed toy tea sets, from left: Dolly Dingle set, although dated on box 1983, the style and marking is more like 1960s and the same set may have been made for several decades, includes two cups and saucers, distributed by company in Shackman, New York, marked "Made in Japan" ($30); floral set with boy and girl on box, marked "Made in Japan," c1970s ($28).

From left: German bear motif, round teapot is probably from a set, no mark, made in Germany, modern ($18); boxed set, Reutter, made in Germany, hand-painted detail, most pieces not marked, modern ($30).

Holly Hobbie with her tea set, marked "Made In Japan," sets says: "Friends are Fun," part of 15-piece boxed set ($55 with box). Holly Hobbie doll is named Heather, c1970s, American Greetings ($22).

Children's and Toy Teapots & Tea Sets

ITEM	VALUE
Akro Agate, glass set, interior panel, 15-21 pieces with lids, 1940s-1951, USA	$150.00-$225.00
Aluminum, red handle and finial, teapot only	$28.00
American flag and chicks, teapot, sugar and creamer, mark "Hand-Painted Nippon"	$95.00
Bears, playing sports, set with 6 place-settings, Japan	$275.00-$325.00
Blue Willow, china, set with 4 place settings, mark Made in Japan, c1950s-1960s	$95.00-$130.00
Blue Willow, paneled willow, marked "Real Staffordshire Willow, Henry Alcock & Co.," c1900	$350.00-$400.00
Bye-Baby Bunting, baby, animals, rhymes, set with 4 or 6 place-settings, England, late-1800s	$450.00-$500.00
Chicks, set with 4 place settings, semi-vitreous china, marked "ELPCO, Made in USA," c1900	$400.00
Children, Kate Greenaway design, set with 4 place settings, marked " Cleve-Ron China USA"	$350.00
Clown children, set with 6 place settings, Castleton China Co., USA, c1940	$250.00
Dutch children in relief as the handles, royal blue, marked "Haarlem," Holland	$150.00-$200.00
Elephant, orange lustre, set with 4 place settings, marked "Made in Japan," c1940s-1950s	$55.00
Geisha girl, set with 4 place settings, orange/red background, marked "Japan"	$95.00
Germany, many versions: flowers, Art Deco, set with 4 place settings, modern	$30.00
Graniteware, set with 4 place settings, USA, some chipping and wear	$75.00
May, scene with girl, made in England, teapot only	$65.00
May, scene with girl, set with 4 place settings, England	$300.00
Mickey Mouse, various 4 place setting sets with lustre, marked "Walt Disney, Made in Japan"	$150.00-$200.00
Nursery Rhymes, gold trim on white porcelain, 6 pieces, England, c1930	$225.00-$300.00
Silver lustre, set with 4 place settings, wear on the silver, made in England, c1920s-1930	$125.00
Silver-plated tea service, Godinger Silver, modern	$40.00
Tin, Dutch scenes, set with 4 place settings, Wolverine Co., USA, 1950s	$110.00
Tin, Little Red Riding Hood or Mother Goose, Ohio Art, no spout, limited pieces, 1940s	$75.00
Tin, Little Red Riding Hood or Three Bears, modern reproduction, shiny tin, USA	$22.00
Wizard of Oz, set with 4 place settings, colorful detail and story lines, modern	$85.00

Figural Teapots

Tina's Cottage, hand-made and hand-painted, this teapot was specially made by Heather Logan, Ceramist, Hollywood, FL. Each teapot is made with different fairies and animals to reflect the individual. A pamphlet explains the artwork behind this teapot including the fact that it shouldn't be used for brewing tea. Note the tea set as a lid finial ($300).

y far, the most popular style of teapot is the figural—those shaped like a person, animal, food or some other thing. Figurals stray as far as possible from the practical to the purely whimsical, while somehow remaining within the confines of teapot characteristics such as a handle, body and spout.

The forerunner of teapots, Korean ewers of the 12th century, were sometimes fashioned after natural items like the lotus flower. This influenced the styles of China and Japan where figural teapots have been made for centuries. Chinese Yixing potters formed many figural earthenware teapots. Although these pots were really works of art, they were designed for practical use. In the 1600s, most teapots in Europe were Chinese export porcelain with figural styles such as hexagonal shapes or those with attached foo dogs.

In the early 1700s, English potters were still trying to invent the right formula for porcelain similar to imported Oriental wares, while producing many earthenware figural teapots such as those like a bundle of bamboo or dragons. Salt-glazing was used to give earthenware a hardness and some of the finest examples were produced from 1720 to 1740, although this technique was used into the next century. Records show English salt-glaze figural teapots from the same period in the shape of a camel, Chinese god or an octagon shape with a view of Portobello captured in 1739 with Admiral Vernon's six ships. While these types of teapots are now museum pieces, it shows the human fascination for projecting our surroundings onto manufactured objects, even teapots.

The fascination with figural teapots has never really diminished although once hard-paste porcelain and china were invented, teapots decorated with every imaginable scene, flower or saying were popular from the late-1700s into the 1800s. With Queen Victoria's influence on tea time, the decorative and ornate teapot with Rococo styling was vogue. Figural teapots weren't part of the traditional Victorian tea time.

By 1850, two movements influenced pottery and porcelain manufacturers and figural teapots were finding a new popularity. The Arts and Crafts Movement touted hand-crafted items which re-

From left: Oriental man and baby, celadon glaze on porcelain, modern, no mark ($28); doughnut style, Oriental teapot, imitation of Canton style, marked "Made in China" ($20).

Oriental garden scene with applied trees and figures, china, paper sticker reads "Ardalt, Japan, Verithin," 8-in. high ($50).

sulted in individualized figural teapots of characters popular in that era or stylized Oriental motifs. The Aesthetic Movement of the 1870s-1890s influenced the whimsical figural styles even into the new century. Out of England came Toby-styled teapots, Dickens' characters and teapots such as the ever-popular Minton "fish swallowing a fish." During this same period, Royal Worcester produced a figural depicting Oscar Wilde.

From the late-1800s into the early-1900s, Japanese Banko teapots became more popular. This was fueled by the 1878 Paris Exhibition where quite a number of Banko potteries were represented. While not all Banko ware teapots are figurals, some recognizable shapes include a bird, duck and a god of many faces (teapot with 7 different faces).

From the 1930s-1950s a range of subjects were fashioned into teapots. Japan exported dragon ware and all sorts of animals. English teapots in the shape of people, houses and nursery characters abounded. At the same time, figural teapots were mass-produced from Germany, England and Japan. U.S. potteries realized the market for whimsical items and companies like Red Wing, Hall China and Bauer designed figural pots like a rooster, donut and boat shape, respectively.

A decline in figural teapots was seen during the late-1960s and 1970s, but popularity in the last two decades has steadily grown. Collectors specializing in figural teapots find the selections are almost endless, but keep an eye out for those vessels produced before 1960. Modern figural teapots made in China, Taiwan and Japan can be recognized by their white ceramic body. Those produced in England will have marks from well-known names such as Martin Bibby, Tony Wood and the Carter Studio. Fitz & Floyd have designed and marketed beautiful teapots manufactured in the Orient during the last two

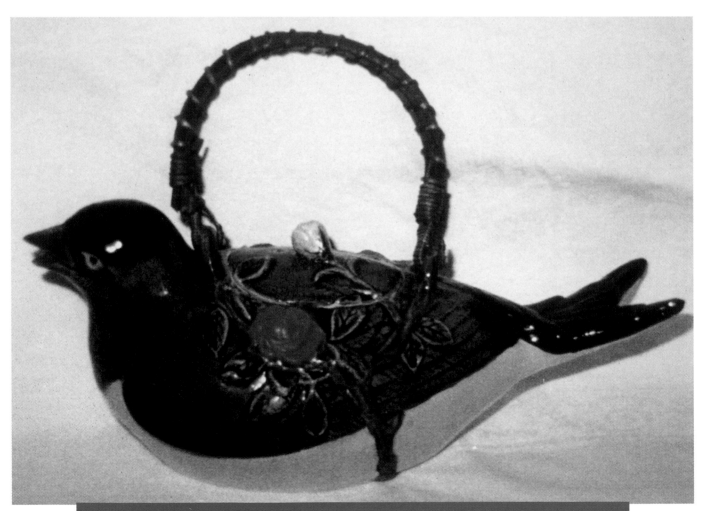

Banko teapot, bisque clay, details hand-painted, wicker bail handle, made in Japan (95).

decades. Many of these new teapots demand higher prices than some vintage examples on the secondary market. Collectors realize that even new shapes may only be produced for a limited time and won't want to pass up a design that has piqued their interest.

The trend in collecting figural teapots is to concentrate on those pots made by a particular designer. An example is the popularity of various sized figurals by Paul Cardew. A Cardew Collectors Club was established in 1995 and has addresses in the United States and England. While modern teapots normally have new marks and are made from a lighter porcelain, collectors need to be aware of reproductions, especially blue and white shapes made in and marked "China."

While figurals may not be every collector's cup of tea, even traditional enthusiasts maybe unable to resist a special teapot shaped like Humpty Dumpty or a majolica styled monkey.

Limited Edition, Cardew design along with box designed like tea crate, Donald Duck is stuck in a wringer washer, titled Donald Mangle, numbered and dated on bottom ($125).

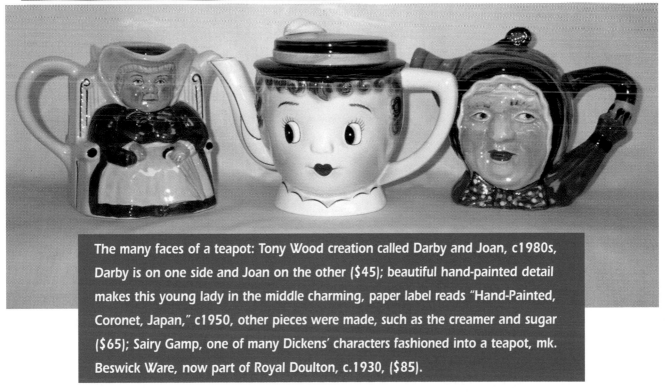

The many faces of a teapot: Tony Wood creation called Darby and Joan, c1980s, Darby is on one side and Joan on the other ($45); beautiful hand-painted detail makes this young lady in the middle charming, paper label reads "Hand-Painted, Coronet, Japan," c1950, other pieces were made, such as the creamer and sugar ($65); Sairy Gamp, one of many Dickens' characters fashioned into a teapot, mk. Beswick Ware, now part of Royal Doulton, c.1930, ($85).

Banko teapot, wicker bail handle, detailed hand-painting, lid fits smooth enough to blend in with the design, duck has molded feet on bottom of pot ($120).

Bottom of Banko teapot shows that the molded design of the feet of this duck.

YIXING TEAPOTS

The earliest known teapots were small, delicate vessels not much larger than the cups (or bowls) previously used to steep tea and some of the finest examples are from the village of Yixing, China. With an artful diligence, the skilled potters of Yixing have been a continual influence in the world of earthenware clay for five centuries. Stoneware teapots, and other items, were crafted for regional use since the 1500s but exportation increased the 1600s from the I-Hsing area (modern spelling is Yixing and pronounced "yee shing").

Situated west of Shanghai in the Jaingsu province near Lake Tai, this area has yielded her "purple sand" or zishayao to the many factories and artisans in a process that has changed minimally over time. The varying degrees of iron in the clay determine the color, and the general term for all hues is called zisha, but the most sought after is the purplish clay.

This clay is considered superior for brewing tea because of its heat retaining and porous properties, allowing for absorption of the tea to "season" the pot. Yixing aficionados prize those pots which have a built-up patina on the inside of the pot from continual steeping of tea. A teapot is seasoned with only a certain blend of tea, thus reserving several pots for particular varieties. These small pots are not washed with soap or other cleaning agents but rinsed with water and toweled dry.

Each pot is formed and pieced by a single potter. Clay is prepared in sheets where sections such as the body, handle and spout are cut, joined and shaped with great attention to detail. The lid is cut from the same piece of clay for the body, allowing for an exact fit even after firing. The strong properties of this clay, one of which is a low shrinkage rate during firing, has long been the envy of European potters. Yixing teapots are stamped or marked with the artisan's seal bearing their name, referred to as a "chop mark." This stamp can be found on the underside of a teapot but sometimes is placed in unusual places such as under the lid, on top of the lid, or on the body near the handle.

Although Yixing teapots are formed from an earthen clay, these natural colored vessels are really a stoneware, strengthened and hardened by firing at low temperatures for a finished piece that can withstand the heat of boiling water. Yixing ware is not glazed, revealing the smooth-textured beautiful clay and allowing for seasoning of the pot. If a glaze is applied, such as a clear coat to the inside of the pot, some collectors consider the pot unsuitable for anything other than display.

The Chinese culture is filled with respect for nature and a symbolism representing its legends, surroundings and lore. These red, brown, ochre or black teapots reflect this symbolism in design. Some depict seasonal changes, others are shaped like the mystical lotus flower or inscribed with Chinese poetry and writing, imparting wishes of happiness, luck and fortune to the tea drinker. Other shapes imitate fruit or bear finials of animals such as a rabbit representing the story of the jade hare. Octagonal, pear and squatty round shapes can also be found with added detail such as twigs for handles or a dragon head as the spout. Artisans may apply decoration such as leaves, flowers, bamboo or delicate painted detail. These teapots are never gaudy or extreme and even modern versions hold to artistic detail and hand-craftsmanship.

In the 1600s, these wonderful little teapots were exported to Holland, then, not long afterward, to England. At this time in Europe, tea was still considered medicinal and the small teapots were perfect for one or two people. It wasn't long before Dutch and English potters began to imitate Yixing teapots and those from the late-1600s and early-1700s reflect this desire. Examples of Yixing teapots from the late-1700s are rare, viewed in museums or publicly displayed private collections.

Modern Yixing teapots may be replicas of vintage designs or reflect contemporary ideas but individual character shines through each piece of art. In the United States, Yixing teapots have been growing in popularity among collectors in the last decade. A heightened awareness of their exquisite characteristics has seen prices soar from $40 to hundreds of dollars for new examples. A recent Internet web site had three different, modern Yixing teapots listed for sale at $850 to $1,500, although these were unexpectedly high prices. Rare blue colors from early-19th century or a compressed globular shape from the 18th century may command the above prices. New Yixing teapots can still be found for $55-$75 or even less in tea shops and import stores.

If you're fortunate enough to add a Yixing teapot to your collection, you may resolve that it's too special for tea even if it was designed for that special "seasoned" purpose.

From left: Cottage, marked "Ye Olde Cottage, Price Kensington, Made in England," c1930-1950s ($55); cottage, paper label "Stylecraft Quality Ceramic, Bradshaw Int'l, Calif.," Japan, c1970s ($30).

From left: The Olde Mill, 2-cup, modern, shape of mill, marked "Sadler, England" with description ($35); Tudor House, English Country Houses series, marked "Sadler, England" with description ($35).

From left: The Old Forge, part of English Country Crafts series, marked "Sadler, England" with description, modern ($35); castle, part of Camelot Castle series, marked "Sadler, England," modern ($35).

House furnishings have become a favorite subject for figurals. Porcelain fireplace and comfy chair both marked and made in Taiwan, modern ($22 each).

Cottage set includes creamer, teapot, covered sugar, hand-painted detail, marked "Made in Japan," c1950s ($55 set).

Evidence of travel should be the name for this trunk and suitcase teapot made by Martin Bibby of Swineside Ceramics in England, artist gives special attention to detail on his many figural teapots, modern ($85). (photo courtesy of Gary Stotsky, Pennsylvania)

From left: Birthday cake, modern, marked "Lillian Vernon, Made in Taiwan" ($22); carousel horse, modern, marked "Heritage Mint Ltd.," made in Taiwan ($25).

From left: Smiling sailor, pastel colors, marked "Japan," c1950s ($55, matching salt and pepper $25); salt and pepper walking teapots, similar to Jack and Jill characters, marked paper label "Kelvin, Hand-Painted, Japan," c1950s ($28); capped man, Scottie teapot, marked "Wade, Made in England," hand-painted, 1953-1955 ($85).

Fruity teapots, from left: Red apple has wonderful air-brushed type detail with glossy glaze, no mark, c1950 ($30); yellow apple and matching creamer, hand-painted detail, bisque type body, no mark, c1930 ($55 set).

From left: Bluebird, popular 1950s cheerful figure, made in Japan and distributed by Lefton China Co., paper sticker on side ($75); beckoning poodle in a soft-matte glaze and pastel colors, marked "Japan," c1950s-1960s, other matching pieces made ($45).

Similar to Elsie the Cow, interesting body that is from same mold as the bunny teapot next to it, notice the thumping foot, both marked "Japan," late-1950s ($20 each).

From left: Duck has frog hitching a ride, no mark, made in Japan ($35); snail in bright yellow, "Japan" impressed into porcelain, c1970s ($35).

From left: Elephant is carrying an elephant on this hand-painted small pot, marked "Made in China," c1970 ($22); This alligator has been eating well, small ceramic pot is hand-painted, no mark, possibly souvenir from a Southern state ($18).

From left: Tea bag pot, brown glaze, "Sylvac, Made in England" impressed into pottery, c1960 ($35); elephant set, unusual interpretation with elephant head for spout and another for handle, patchwork design, even inside teapot, marked "Leslie Furlong," individual ceramics project, great for kids' tea time, especially with boys, c1980 ($40 for the set).

Elephant with metal bail handle, hand-painted Howdah (man riding) and design, marked "Japan" and "CG" which stands for Chungai, c1940s-1950s ($85).

Dancing kitties, modern, made in Korea, mark includes "Applause, Inc. of Woodland Hills, California," one in a series offered, spout not practical for tea ($30).

Black and white cat is a favorite figural, paper sticker reads "Cortendorf, West Germany," backstamp on bottom with same, hand-painted detail ($95).

From left: Trio of beckoning cats, from left: White china and typical orange-red flowers, marked Taiwan ($22); black glaze, painted detail over the glaze, c1950s, possibly part of stacking set ($30); white china, holding the catch of the day, marked "made in China" ($28).

Pirate is Long John Silver, marked "Royal Doulton, c1989, England" ($95). (photo courtesy of Gary Stotsky, Pennsylvania)

Toby teapot, many versions have been created, this colorful one with legs as spout and handle, marked "made in England" ($65). (photo courtesy of Gary Stotsky, Pennsylvania)

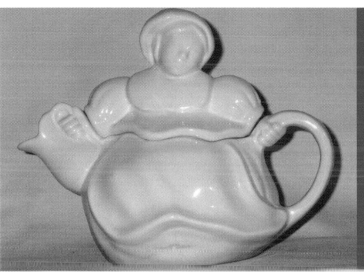

Dutch maid, jug is spout, "Redwing, U.S.A." impressed into pottery, c1940 ($120).

Conch shell is made in style similar to majolica, rough molding gives realistic detail, no mark, made in Japan, other pieces made with souvenir markings, c1950 ($45).

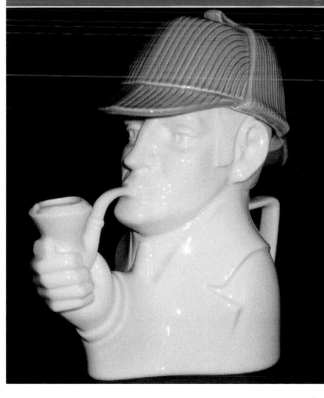

Sherlock Holmes, large teapot individually commissioned by Dan Brasier in 1988 to be made by the Hall China company. Also marked with the designer's name, Don Schreckengost. Teapot is a little heavy for tea but great as a conversation pieces. Paper pamphlet included with pot ($250).

From left: Clowning around with tea, this cheerful guy has tea written on his hat, bail handle, c1950s, marked "Made in Japan" ($28); black glaze, painted detail over glaze, some wear, part of stacking cozy set, paper sticker and backstamp, Thames, Japan ($32).

From left: Pillsbury Doughboy brings cookies to your tea time! Marked "Benjamin & Medwin Inc. NY, NY, 1997, The Pillsbury Co., Made in China" ($40); friar, cross-eyed, only marked is some numbers, imitation Goebel, c1950s ($45).

From left: Butler will keep your tea bags for you, hand-painted design on porcelain, tea bags can be pulled out at base, modern, although has the look of 1950s, made in Taiwan ($28); maid from 1970s, marked "Eda, Mann, An Eda Original" with sticker that says "Mann, Japan" ($40).

Black piano ready to add a tune to your tea time, except that it doesn't have a music box, lid is the bouquet on top, impressed "Made in China," c1980s ($25).

A prop(er) tea can be served in this airplane, from left: T4-2, driven by a terrier, marked "Mann, Japan," impressed with the same, by Eda Mann, 1970s ($35); S.S. Tea bi-plane will give tea another ride, marketed by Fitz & Floyd, made in Japan, c1970s ($35).

From left: Animated characters decorate this colorful teapot produced by Wade, England for the International Association of Jim Beam Bottle & Specialties Club, 1 of 1700, 1995 ($65); OKT42 will get you there, in this 1978 auto made by Vandor ($45).

White glazed auto, Austin, made by Carlton Ware, England, c1940s ($495). (photo courtesy of The Antique Gallery, Philadelphia)

Silver glazed auto, Morris Minor, made by Carlton Ware, England, c1940s ($495) (photo courtesy of The Antique Gallery, Philadelphia)

Snow White is a crossover collectible for Disney enthusiasts, music box underneath, four of dwarves adorn teapot that plays "Hi-Ho, Hi-Ho," c1940s, made in Japan and marked with "Walt Disney Productions" ($200).

Tom the Piper's Son, made by the Shawnee Pottery Co., U.S.A, decorated in various styles, those with gold trim and plenty of hand-painted detail demand higher prices, this example ($150-$200). Others with glazed colored body ($85-$125).

Figural Teapots

ITEM	VALUE
Auto, bubble car, designed by Martin Bibby, Swineside Ceramics, England, modern	$75.00
Blue bird, Banko ware, rattan handle, hand-painted rose vine, relief, no mark, c1920-1930s	$95.00
Bunny, pottery versions made by both Sadler & Sylvac, England, c1930s-1940s	$85.00-125.00
Camel, sitting, Banko ware, rattan handle, no mark, Japanese, c1920s-1930s	$110.00
Cameo shape, gold detail, various scenes in cameo, James Sadler & Sons, c1950	$95.00
Cat, beckoning brown and white Siamese, marked "Tony Wood, England," c1960s	$65.00
Cat, white Persian, ribbon forms handle, rose at neck is spout, by Fitz & Floyd, modern	$65.00
Cats, dancing couple, from series by Applause, California, made in Korea, modern	$35.00
Cinderella, teapot is coach, figures in relief, gold detail, Ellgreave, England, c1950	$85.00-$125.00
Cow, black and white with red boots, designed by Fiona Stokes, Otagiri, Japan, modern	$55.00
Crinoline lady, made in variety of pastel colors, Sadler, England, c1930	$95.00
Dog, beckoning bulldog, black and white, no mark, possibly German, c1960s-1970s	$60.00
Dog, beckoning hound in dark colors, marked "Erphilla, Germany," c1940s-1950s	$75.00
Donut, Chinese red color by Hall China, USA, c1930s-1950s	$250.00
Dragon ware, detailed dragon spout, handle, finial, heavy gold, Satsuma, Japan, c1880	$2,200.00
Faces, Seven Gods of Wisdom, Banko, rattan handle, mark in Japanese writing, c1900	$250.00
Frog, holding a lily flower, ceramic, one in series "Freda & Freddie," Otagiri, Japan	$45.00
Granny Ann, multi-colored, Shawnee Pottery Co., marked "Pat. USA & Granny Ann"	$130.00
House, Victorian style, Village tea room by Lenox, part of series, marked "Taiwan," 1991	$85.00
Humpty Dumpty, many colors, sugar & creamer available, Lingard, England, c1930	$125.00
Kitten, wearing a hat, head only, blue around face, marked with numbers, "Lefton, Japan"	$95.00-$135.00
Lady, sitting to pour jug, babushka is lid, by Sitzendorf, late-1880s	$800.00
Little Old Lady, hand-painted decoration, H.J. Wood, England, c1930-1950s	$85.00-$125.00
Little Old Lady, hand-painted decoration, Queensware, England, modern	$65.00-$85.00
Mad Hatter's Tea Party, heart handle, spade spout, England, modern	$95.00
Mary Had a Little Lamb, heavy glaze with gold or silver detail, Lingard, England, c1930	$95.00-$125.00
Mermaid, highly detailed pot by Eliza Hurdle, Bristol, England, modern	$250.00
Old Woman in a Shoe, many colors, sugar & creamer available, Lingard, England, c1930	$125.00
Puzzle pot, porcelain, hand-painted details, no mark, Japanese	$200.00
Quail, part of set, tail is handle, Imari-style decoration, marked "Royal Crown Derby," c1988	$1,000.00
Red Riding Hood, face and hood are lid, Hull pottery company, c1950s-1960s	$365.00
Ronald Reagan, off-white porcelain, Hall China, USA, c1980s	$125.00
Rooster, colorfully hand-painted, tail is handle, Royal Winton, Grimwades, England	$95.00
Sea Shell, large colorful pot by Hull, USA, line called Ebb Tide, c1950s	$400.00
Teepee, Indian is spout, totem pole is handle, marked "Clarice Cliff," late-1940s	$300.00-$500.00
Tom, Tom the Piper's Son, various versions boy with pig, Shawnee, marked "Pat. USA & Tom"	$85.00-$200.00
Tomato, glossy red glaze, no mark possibly Japan or USA, c1950s-1960s	$65.00
Tomato, red matte finish with leaves in relief, matching cups, marked "Made in Japan," 1950	$75.00
Vampire, various manufacturers, made in England, see "Collector's Teapot," modern	$100.00
Watermelon, flower finial, slice shape, marked "Taiwan," modern	$30.00
Whitehouse, flag styling on spout and handle, designer Terry Kerr, marked "Fitz & Floyd"	$100.00
Windmill, hand-painted detail under glaze, marked "Japan," c1940s-1950s	$45.00

Fine China Teapots

Transparent bone china teapots have attracted tea drinkers, brides-to-be and collectors for almost two centuries. And for good reason: Not only is it lightweight and beautiful, it's also strong and durable. China can withstand the boiling hot water for steeping tea and can be decorated in a myriad of ways. The paste from which china is formed can be molded, pressed, cut and even sculpted in the most delicate of patterns. This medium lends itself well to smooth, graceful shapes and to the intricate details of scalloped edges.

Fine china or bone china is one of three types of porcelain which also includes hard-paste and softe paste porcelain (these will be defined in the chapter on porcelain). Bone china is formed first by a hard-paste of kaolin and petuntse. The term kaolin means china clay, from Kao-ling in China where this clay was thought to be first found. Kaolin is formed from decomposing rocks that contain feldspar or aluminum silicate. Kaolin is only found in certain places in the world such as China, Germany, France and England, and that's why most porcelain has been produced in these countries.

Hard-paste porcelain also contains petuntse meaning china stone. This stone has to be finely ground and washed and then is blended with the kaolin and allowed to mature. To produce bone china, the ash of burned animal bones is added to the hard-paste clay. Hard-paste porcelain was first produced in China, and it was over three centuries later before it was perfected in England. During the early-1600s, kaolin was discovered in Japan where potteries soon began producing porcelain. Two of the major china producing areas in Japan are Arita and Kutani.

In Europe, Johann Friedrich Böttger is credited with the invention of porcelain in 1708. After his many attempts, this success was celebrated with the opening of the Royal Saxon Porcelain Manufactory located in Meissen, Germany. In England, some bone china was being produced about 1750, but it wasn't until about 1800 that a

From left: Cup and saucer in the Thousand Faces pattern, transfer design, hand-painted detail, very thin, note flowers inside cup, no mark, made in Japan ($40); Imari design, marked "Gold Imari" with Japanese symbol, "Hand Painted Expressly for Capwells," transfer designs in panels, hand-painting under and over the glaze, c1930s-1950s ($75).

Paneled shape, warming stand, cady and handleless cups, brass bail handle, marked "Japan," cady has a paper label "Hand-crafted in Japan for Lund's Lites, Auburn, WA," c1970s ($75 for all pieces).

From left: Hand-painted Oriental design on an individual sized pot, handle is stationary, matching handleless cup, no mark, possibly Japan or China ($35 for set); Oriental shape like Japanese tea room or house, no mark, fine china with gold butterflies, note the straight spout ($30).

formula was refined by Josiah Spode.

During the same era, transfer printing was invented in England whereby an engraved picture was applied to the surface of china for decoration. Later, transfer printing was done and then the outlined-type scene or picture was hand-painted with other colors. Transfer printing was done both before or after the firing process.

Fine china has a translucent quality and even if you can't see through it when held to the light, you'll find a certain transparency to the body. The process of firing bone ash mixed with hard-paste causes a bonding to take place so there are no separate layers, like glazed pottery, but just a durable body.

Most people relate to fine china or bone china by holding a piece up to the light to test if they can see the shadows of the fingers on the other side. Not all china has the same level of transparency but light can pass through many teapots. By the 1950s, paper labels were added to teapots declaring that they were "bone china." Other backstamps declared the same quality.

From about the late-1920s to the 1950s, dragon ware was produced in Japan and tea cups were fashioned with lithophanes. Geisha girl faces were impressed into the bottoms of tea cups and when the tea was finished, the dainty figure could be seen when held to the light. Lithophanes were not placed in the bottoms of teapots but were definitely a wonderful part of tea time.

Some of the finest hand-painted floral decoration in the world adorns teapots and other tea wares from R.S. Prussia, Germany, Austria and Japan. Blank white bone china has been mass-produced out of these countries for more than a century. The end-result intended for hand-painting by china painters. Passing down particular methods and techniques, china painters use blank white china as their canvas. Many styles and shapes of teapots and tea time accessories have been produced and are still available currently. Brush marks can often be noticed upon close inspection, adding a personal appeal because no two china painted items will be alike.

The Lefton China Company has imported beautiful bone and fine china since the 1940s, mainly from Japan, but since the 1970s, from other Oriental countries. Many Lefton teapots have hand-painted decoration, a fact also stated on some of the backstamps. There is a growing popularity for Lefton China collectibles today, including its teapots. Lefton teapots range from practical round-bodied pots to those with scalloped edges and delicate handles.

Precious Moments tea set, two girls having tea, marked on all pieces "1993, Precious Moments, Inc. Licensee Enesco Corp.," made in China ($90 for set).

From left: Japanese scene with men on a journey, transfer design with hand-painted detail, no mark, made in Japan ($50); Geisha Girl pattern, transfer print with hand-painted detail, marked "Hand-Painted, Made in Japan" with a Japanese house ($75).

Back: Celadon miniature tea set, design is made with rice embedded in clay, when fired, leaves transparent designs, mark is Chinese writing and paper label, made in China ($45); front: Scene of China, restaurant-style ware, reverse side has extensive Chinese writing, marked Kockman, made in China with Chinese lettering in a diamond ($30).

From left: Chinese cloisonné look, Emperor's Red, panels give messages of good luck, prosperity, long life, happiness, marked in Chinese writing and "Made in China" backstamp in red ($75), and the cup and saucer in matching pattern, marked same as pot ($35); Teal green is newer than red of the same pattern, made to look like popular cloisonné, marked in Chinese writing, "Made in China" ($65), and the miniature version of teal teapot, marked same, made for export ($30).

From left: Dragon ware teapot in an air-brushed blue, gold decoration, possibly part of set, marked "H. Katu, Pearl China" in wreath, Nagoya, Japan, c1940s-1950s ($75); Lustre glazes accentuate scene, Art Deco styling, marked "Made in Japan," c1940s ($50).

Pale blue, barrel shape, marked "Rosenthal, Germany," c1960s, note the handle makes for easy gripping ($65). (photo courtesy of Gary Stotsky, Pennsylvania)

From left: Simple beauty, rattan handle, no mark, Oriental manufacture ($35); Belleek, shell and coral pattern called "Limpet Tea Ware," marked in green dates this between 1946 and 1955 ($150).

Gold-trim two-tone, marked "Japan," note tiny spout, c1930s ($50). (photo courtesy of Gary Stotsky, Pennsylvania)

Bamboo leaves, black panel and temple scene are part of this set, which has a lid on the creamer, as well as the sugar, marked "Made in Japan" in gold, late-1950s to 1960s ($55 for the set).

Noritake set, eight cups and saucers, sugar and creamer, teapot, mark includes pattern name "Jania" with "N" in wreath, "U.S. design pat. pend.," lightweight ($85 for set).

Fine China Teapots

ITEM	VALUE
Belleek, shamrock pattern, green modern mark includes name Belleek, c1970s-1990s	$225.00
Belleek, shell pattern with shamrocks, handle is Irish harp, marked "Belleek," modern	$125.00
Belleek, thistle pattern, white, black mark with wrap-around banner, c1950	$250.00
Blue Canton style, reproduction by Historic Charleston Foundation, Mottehedah, 1977	$120.00
Blue Net pattern, all-over cobalt and gold over white, Russian Lomonosov, modern	$125.00
Blue Willow, with gold, by Royal Doulton, England, marked "Booth's Real Olde Willow," c1981	$175.00
Castellon pattern, red and black modern design, marked "Villeroy & Boch," c1990	$150.00
Cobalt body and lid, Katherine pattern, gold, marked crown, shield, German words	$150.00
Fern and berries decor on white bone china, marked "Wedgwood, Made in England," c1930	$150.00-$200.00
Floral, hand-painted roses, loop in handle, marked "Handpainted, Japan," diamonds and TT	$95.00
Gold trim on white, flower finial, 6 cup, Golden Edge pattern by Herend, marked "Hungary"	$130.00
Heritage teapot, pale green with roses and gold, hand-decorated, England, modern	$75.00
Imari pattern, Coalport teapot, London shape variation, early-1800s	$1,500.00
Individual-sized pot, set tea for two, robin's egg blue and gold, marked "Noritake"	$45.00
Japanese lantern shape, texture under glaze, 1-piece reed handle, no mark, Japanese	$40.00
Minton, new oval shape, monochrome scene, hand-painted, early-1800s	$350.00-$500.00
Modern decor, designed by Roy Lichtenstein, Rosenthal China, Germany, c1984	$200.00
Moss Rose pattern, scalloped design, marked "Rosenthal, Germany," c1950	$175.00
Old Imari pattern, traditional design in red, cobalt and gold, Royal Crown Derby, modern	$900.00
Oriental motif, red and gold design, reed wrapped handle, marked under lid "Hasimoto China"	$35.00
Oriental motif, white china, one-piece reed handle, spout cut-away, marked in Japanese writing.	$35.00
Pembroke pattern china, bird and flowers, oval shape, marked "Aynsley, England"	$185.00
Phoenix Bird pattern, blue and white, individual size, marked "Japan"	$65.00
Pink pearlized lustre, oblong shape, dogwood blossoms, R.S. Prussia, no mark	$350.00
Ribbed shape, Oriental shape and decor, 4 cup, marked "Japan"	$45.00
Royal Copenhagen, Floral Danica pattern, 8-cup, hand-painted, 24K trim	$2,800.00
Royal Creamware, pierced teapot, intricate, soft cream color, marked with name, modern	$110.00
Royal Creamware, reproductions from 18th century, Victoria & Albert Museum, marked, 1995	$100.00
Side handle, straight spout, tapered shape with sprigs of flowers, no mark, possibly German	$135.00
Susie Cooper Corn Poppy pattern, by Wedgwood, c1960s-1970s	$85.00-$95.00
White and gold pattern, tapered shape, heavy gold, part of service for 12, marked "Noritake"	$55.00
White with gold trim, individual size, large creamer, sugar, Bavarian Germany set	$65.00
Winter tree trunk scene, pastel blue section, diamond shape, marked "M.P. China" (Japan)	$55.00
Worcester, Japan Star pattern, cobalt, red and gold decor, tilted finial, late-1700s	$750.00
White with purple flowers, rattan bail handle, label and marked "Asuka, Fine China, Japan"	$30.00

Floral Teapots

Floral teapots have been the traditional choice of tea time for centuries where roses, pansies, black-eyed Susans or a bouquets of mixed flowers have graced many a table. Crossing gender preferences, continents and countries, the universal appeal of floral teapots has been used on every type of material from which teapots have been formed.

Floral teapots are often associated with English porcelain and Victorian tea time, but flowers have decorated teapots from the 12th century Korean ewers. Chinese export porcelain was highly decorated with an array of flowering patterns. Japanese Imari and Banko styles incorporated flowers in decoration. Early American enamelware, silver and silver-plated, majolica and pottery teapots are just a sampling of the many types of pots on which flowers have been used to lure tea drinkers.

This chapter will concentrate on pottery, porcelain and china teapots because the floral decoration on these pots has evolved over the centuries into four distinct methods of decoration. When arranging tea time today, it's vogue to mix and match similar patterns or contrasting colors. By using floral teapots and accessories, this can be easily done with a charming effect. Similar floral patterns were used by different companies.

A long-standing favorite is the Moss Rose design which is a spray of reddish-pink roses with mossy stems. Slightly differing versions have been produced in England, France and Germany. In the United States, the Wheeling Pottery

Tea set made by and marked "Sadler," a popular pattern of swirl-shaped body, tiny roses connected with gold, sugar bowl has no lid (common in English tea sets), 1940s-1950s ($95 for set).

Company (Wheeling, WV) produced a best-selling Moss Rose pattern dinnerware from the late-1800s until 1910. A widely recognized Moss Rose pattern has been produced by the Rosenthal Porcelain Factory in Bavaria and by many companies in Japan and China. Collectors need to study this popular pattern because it's still being produced today on low-quality items from China and Taiwan. Many sizes of children's tea sets were made with Moss Rose decoration. A multi-piece set was made in Japan during the 1940s and 1950s. A smaller set was recently offered by a mail order company.

Moss Rose is just one example of popular floral teapot and tea set themes. Others include cabbage roses or a large red rose called England's Rose. Major porcelain- and china-producing companies in England made beautiful floral teapots since the

From left: Modern lines, possibly part of set, marked with paper label "Sterling China, Japan," late-1950s, early 1960s ($35); Moss Rose pattern, 2-3 cup, marked "Japan" in gold and paper label "Apex Quality, Japan," c1960s ($35).

Back: Soft pink glaze unusual, oval shape, mark raised in clay "Sadler, England," c1950 ($65); oval and ribbed shape, Georgian pattern by Arthur Wood, mark includes name, banner over globe "Quality, Made in England," c1940 ($65).

late-1800s. The James Sadler & Sons Company made its first teapot in 1882 and has steadily provided the world with excellent tea vessels. One of the world's largest ceramic teapot producers, Sadler pots are easy to find on the secondary market and available new from certain retailers. They've set the standard for floral teapots with many styles and shapes available, including a classic shape called Park Lane, which has a swirled body and decorated in many floral patterns. One pattern the company has produced for many years is decorated with tiny pink roses connected by gold to form a diamond or net design. This has also been available with a music box.

Sadler teapots were first produced in a brown

Two floral Ellgreave teapots, representation of the various styles produced in porcelain by the Ellgreave company, a Division of Woods and Sons (from left): burgundy roses marked with red and black backstamp, similar to British Royal Arms mark; daisy pattern pot, impressed with "Ellgreave, England." Teapots are valued at $55 each.

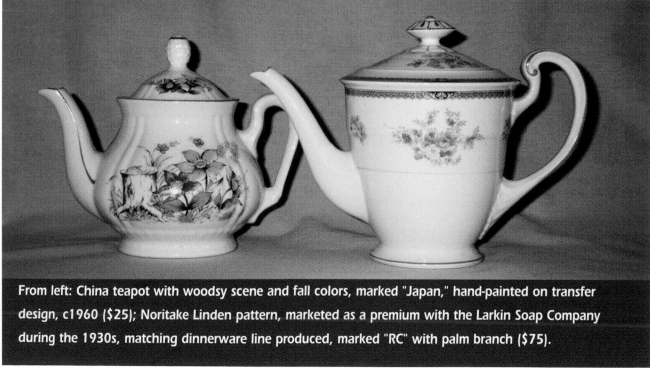

From left: China teapot with woodsy scene and fall colors, marked "Japan," hand-painted on transfer design, c1960 ($25); Noritake Linden pattern, marketed as a premium with the Larkin Soap Company during the 1930s, matching dinnerware line produced, marked "RC" with palm branch ($75).

bodied clay; after 1960, a white clay was used. Its backstamp is a called "Crown Ribbon" and has been used since 1935. Marks on its floral teapots also include raised lettering of Sadler and England. A classic floral shape called Heritage has six sides and the upper half of the pot is decorated in several colorful floral patterns.

Offset Designs—Transfer Printed Teapots

Transfer printing is a process by which a design is applied to the china or porcelain glaze. First used in the 1700s, the design was engraved on a copper plate, inked and then transferred to thin paper. Then it could be applied to the shapes and

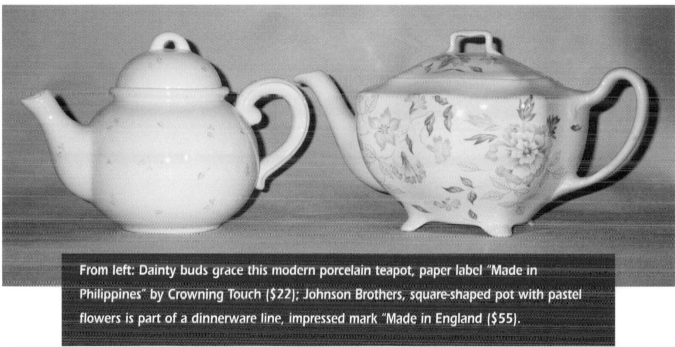

From left: Dainty buds grace this modern porcelain teapot, paper label "Made in Philippines" by Crowning Touch ($22); Johnson Brothers, square-shaped pot with pastel flowers is part of a dinnerware line, impressed mark "Made in England ($55).

From left: Cobalt with gold flowers, pamphlet attached, impressed mark "Chatsworth, Made in England," backstamp in gold for Arthur Wood, c1930 ($95, with pamphlet); blue underglaze pattern, electric pot, paper label "Original Arnart Creation Japan," c1950s ($30).

If you've never held a tea time before, you're missing a particular treat, and it's easier than you think. You'll enjoy tea with friends or family more frequently if you keep things simple at first and gradually add little pleasures to this time of respite. Today, tradition has been thrown out the window and any kind of tea, food or dishes are acceptable—ambiance is more important.

Tea time can be managed comfortably regarding preparation, serving up the tea and enjoying the companionship if you limit your group to three or four people. Allow enough time for rejuvenation without infringing upon daily schedules. Tea time can be planned for any time of the day.

Tea Time Basics.

Pick a favorite tea. If it's loose tea, you'll need a strainer and they come in versions of two basic types: a tea ball or infuser filled with tea and placed inside the pot to steep and then removed, or the type which is used when loose tea is infused directly into the pot and poured off through a strainer into each cup. Either type requires a holder or small dish in which to place them after use.

There are many quality teas available in convenient tea bags although many a tea connoisseur would never consider such a thing. Bagged teas range anywhere from the well-known brands such as Lipton, Tetley and Red Rose to wonderful flavored teas like ginger peach by The Republic of Tea or fruit and vanilla flavored teas by Fortunes (which are packed in small wooden boxes). If you're new to tea, I encourage using a bagged tea and once you've gained some confidence, try brewing a loose blend.

Select a round bodied teapot that pours without dripping. Give it a test first. If you have a favorite pot that consistently drips, you may want to purchase "drip catchers" available at tea shops. There are a couple styles—one is disposable paper slipped onto the spout, another is an attached type of foam to catch drips.

You'll need a tea kettle for boiling the water. Choose one with a whistle that lets you know when it's ready. Enamel lined or steel tea kettles are recommended—other metals will impart unwanted flavors into the water.

Before your first tea time with a guest or two, experiment with making a pot of tea. Try adding lemon or cream to black tea, honey to flavored teas or cream and sugar. Everyone's tastes vary with the type of tea and sweeteners or added flavoring, so try different combinations to determine what works well. For guests, it's best to have a choice of these additional tea flavorings but recommend your favorite.

Tea time dishes include cups and saucers and teaspoons. Place one spoon in the sugar bowl and another for each participant. Cups and saucers don't have to be fancy or delicate china, although they are more festive and it's vogue to mix and match patterns. Collectible hostess sets are becoming increasingly popular. These sets are dessert plates with the saucer-type rim for placing your tea cup and some even have a molded thumb grip for balancing. On occasion, a set can be found with the creamer, sugar and teapot.

curves of a piece like a teapot. The most common transfer printing was done in black. As the process became more common, hand-painted color was added to the transferred outline. Quite elaborate floral displays were transfer-printed onto teapots such as the Japanese Imari and Satsuma.

While the methods used in transfer printing may have streamlined, it was used into the 20th century. Modern methods use machines for this process similar to offset printing. One of the advantages of using an interim step prevents the image from being applied backwards—which would happen if done directly.

In transfer printing, the teapot has to be fired a second time at a lower temperature to bond the transferred design and any added decoration. Teapots painted with a floral decor over the glaze in the 1950s and 1960s were not fired a second time and this paint easily chips or washes off (to the dismay of collectors). Today, permanent inks and special chemical bonding does not require a second firing to always set the image.

In the United States, England and Europe, this method is referred to as transfer printing; in the Orient it's called stenciling. When you find a transfer printed item, you'll be able to actually feel the image on the teapot.

Artists in Residence — Factory Hand-Painted Teapots

Once mass-production was used to make teapots, decorators and artists were employed to put the finishing artwork on floral teapots. If a teapot uses the term "hand-painted" in the back-stamp or mark, don't trust that the total design was hand-done. The term "hand-painted" was used as a selling point, even if it only referred to the gold decoration on the teapot. Look for brush strokes that are often easy to notice on floral teapots, and you'll know it was hand-painted.

Factories found different methods to help speed up the hand-painting they desired on pottery, porcelain or china. One way was to have slight indentations formed in the mold, designating where a floral spray should be painted. Weil Ware, a California pottery company producing floral dinnerware lines during the 1940s and 1950s, used indentations for decoration on its ware. Barely noticeable, when running your fingers over a teapot or cup and saucer, you can feel this difference along with noticing the variations in brush strokes.

From left: Cup and saucer, similar to pattern of teapot, marked "Lefton China," saucer also has red and gold sticker ($45); floral decal and transfer designs in gold, white china, no mark, Japan, c1950 ($40).

TEA TIME TIPS

Planning a tea. Set a date and time, invite friends or family and then begin planning. The invitation can simply be done by phone but for special occasion teas, a tea-themed invitation is charming and can be found In tea shops or other stores. The main things to consider are the tea, the food and the atmosphere.

If your guests are seasoned tea drinkers, ask about their preferences. Favorites include black teas, such as Darjeeling, or a green tea like Jasmine. But if you want to surprise them, pick up a lightly flavored tea. It's always amazing to introduce someone to tea and one of my favorites is called "Celebration Blend" from Fluer de Tea here in San Diego and can be mail ordered. It's a black tea with orange and spices blended enough for flavor but not to be overpowering. A specialty food market, such as Trader Joe's, carry a variety of loose and bagged tea, including a wonderful bulk tea called Real Earth Blend. There are many fine mail order tea companies and it's fun to try different flavors. (See the Reference Section.)

Because teapots aren't typically large and everyone will be enjoying their tea, be prepared to steep at least two pots of tea. After serving the first cups, fill the kettle with fresh water and put it on to boil again. You may even want to brew two kinds of tea in different teapots.

When planning a tea time menu, keep it simple so that you are not exhausted in preparation and can enjoy the fellowship. It's helpful if most of the food can be at least partially prepared ahead of time and then assembled or set out for tea. When you're awaiting the ring of a doorbell, you'll only need to be setting the kettle to boil and arranging the place settings.

Almost anything goes when deciding upon a tea time menu—from merely a selection of cookies to croissant sandwiches, fruit and a colorful trifle. (See the Reference Section for good books on tea time filled with recipe ideas and a wealth of other suggestions.)

Play instrumental music, light a pretty candle or set out a bouquet of flowers to create a welcoming atmosphere, realizing that tea can be taken in the kitchen, dining room or living room. Once tea has been served, guests will appreciate a focus other than just gossipy news. Be prepared to have a poem to read, a funny anecdote or an interesting newspaper article.

The most enjoyable tea times are often done impromptu, but special occasion teas require more advanced planning. A birthday or Christmas tea require special menu ingredients or washing of a favorite tea set and possibly finding a table favor for each person. This can be as simple as a bookmark, special chocolate candy or poem printed on pretty paper. More expensive ideas would be a gift book such as one on tea or teapots, a special cup and saucer to use and then take home or a tea spoon.

Hostessing a tea doesn't require a special occasion, but it will feel like one when you bring out a beautiful teapot, steep some flavorful tea and enjoy a tradition that's been practiced for almost four centuries.

The Arts and Crafts Movement influenced the trend for individually designed and decorated items in potteries. This carried well into the 20th century when many well-known designers were employed by potteries. Most pieces done by these artists will be marked and some names to watch for include Clarice Cliff, Susie Cooper, Rockwell Kent and Don Blanding. Others formed their own potteries such as Sascha Brastoff. In many cases, these artists had others working under their direction although the well-known name will be the only one to appear on a teapot.

Teapots that were hand-decorated in the factory with delicate to bright and gaudy floral decorations carry a special appeal because of the hand-craftsmanship used. More and more, items are produced in one place and shipped to Malaysia or other areas for hand-decorating. Collectors appreciate the time-consuming work that went into factory hand-painted teapots, knowing that one day it may be a thing of the past and completely automated.

Special Strokes — Hand-Painted or China Painted Teapots

Painting on blank white china was inspired from the decorations on porcelain from Meissen, Capodimonte and Sevres of 200 years ago. Artists today employ similar methods, only the use of advanced type of paints, thinners and liquid gold have changed to ease this process.

Many artists have so perfected their style that at first you may not realize a floral spray on your teapot was actually done by a china painter. A

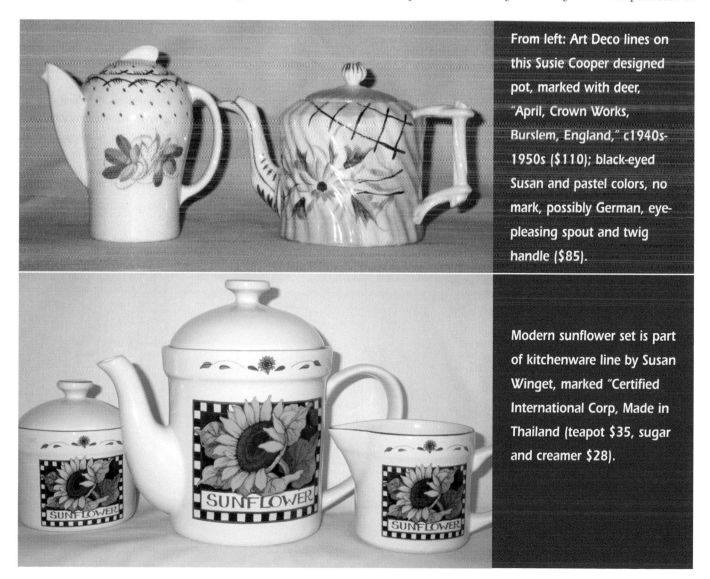

From left: Art Deco lines on this Susie Cooper designed pot, marked with deer, "April, Crown Works, Burslem, England," c1940s-1950s ($110); black-eyed Susan and pastel colors, no mark, possibly German, eye-pleasing spout and twig handle ($85).

Modern sunflower set is part of kitchenware line by Susan Winget, marked "Certified International Corp, Made in Thailand (teapot $35, sugar and creamer $28).

source of distinction are tiny brush strokes or the signature on the underside of the piece. Gold trim is painted with a banding wheel which allows the pot to be turned evenly while the artist steadily applies gold. On handles or spouts, trim must be applied without a guide and this application is an art in itself, requiring a steady hand and even working of the brush.

There are china painting books, classes and regional associations where those interested can learn this wonderful art. China painters often hold shows where you can purchase either the blanks or the fully decorated items. Blanks are available from many countries in several parts of the world: China, Japan, Germany, Bavaria and England.

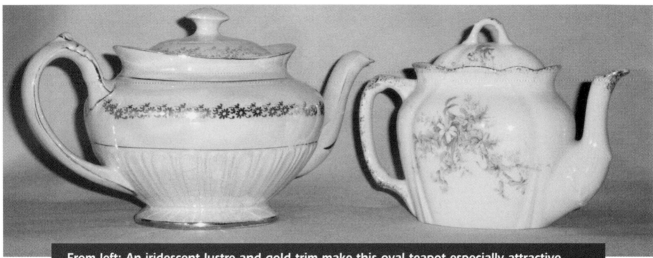

From left: An iridescent lustre and gold trim make this oval teapot especially attractive, mark is a wreath with "DC" and "Made in Poland," c1920 ($95); the slim shape of this china pot is unusual, applied decal, marked "Victoria, Carlsbad, Austria," c1930 ($80).

Weil Ware, pattern named Rose, with brown roses, hand-painted, marked with name and donkey, late-1940s to 1950s ($75, matching creamer and sugar is $50 for set).

Mass-Production — Applied Decal Flowers

Modern factory production necessitates methods that are quick and applying a decal type decoration to a teapot has been used since the late-1800s. Both wet and dry methods of application have been used through the years. Today, machines can apply a decal design to a teapot before or after the glaze.

While decals make production faster, the appeal of hand-decoration is also a strong selling point. After a floral decal was applied to a teapot, in many cases, a special touch was added with hand-painted detail or slip. Teapots with minimum hand-applied detail are sometimes marked "hand-painted." While it's true that a small amount of gold or touches of paint were added to an applied floral design, the words "hand-painted" shouldn't mislead collectors today into believing the whole design was hand done.

One of the hottest floral teapots collected today is chintz ware. Produced by many companies (predominantly in England), this calico-type pattern is bright and cheerful. In fact, it's become so popular with tea time enthusiasts that re-issues of older patterns have been commissioned. *Victoria Magazine* has offered Royal Winton's Wellbeck pattern chintzware since 1998. *Victoria* continually offers additional pieces. A beautiful teapot is available along with all of the pieces needed for tea: creamer, sugar, cups, saucers and dessert plates.

Magnolia Antique Mall in El Cajon, CA, is home to Royal Winton chintz re-issued via Bill and Joanne Hansen. This couple has made several trips to England and recently visited the Royal Winton factory. After some research, they commissioned the company to produce a special

From left: Hand-painted roses, possibly done by china painter, no mark, Germany ($85); hand-painted over transfer-printed design, marked "Austria," 5-in. high, matte finish ($65); delicately scrolled handle and scalloped base, hand-painted over transfer design, marked "Royal Hanover," Germany, late-1920s ($150).

From left: Oriental barrel shape with hand-painted flowers, china, unglazed bottom, no mark, possibly made in China ($35); hand-painted flowers and pastel coloring, note decor on handle, china, no mark, possibly Japan, style similar to Lefton China ($30).

From left: Flower finial, hand-painted daisy-style flowers, marked "Wade Heath England," c1938-1950 ($40); bud finial, hand-painted flowers and details, marked "Booths, Silicon China, Sylvan, Made in England," c1921 ($95).

edition stacking cozy pot and a twin tea break-fast set in the hard to find Joyce-Lynn pattern. Like many other chintz lovers, this couple collects all types of this cheery porcelain and china. (See the Resources Section for a resource on Royal Winton Porcelain.) Founded in 1885, this company in the Stoke-on-Trent area in England is still providing wonderful teapots and other

porcelain to collectors.

Study the types of floral decoration on your teapots and you'll begin to recognize the subtle differences between transfer printing, factory hand-painted, china painted or applied decals. Each has its own appeal and type of detail within the flowers and they all beckon us to a tradition tea time.

Violets are popular with collectors today. From left: Individual-sized pot of china, decal decorated, paper sticker with crown, "Japan, Fine China," late-1950s ($30); china pot with applied violets, marked "Victoria, Carlsbad, Austria" in circle and eagle, not certain if pot had lid as edge is not typically formed for lid ($55); stacking set, decal decorated violets with slip applied, marked "Lefton China" with crown, hand-painted, mark is from the mid-1950s, the sugar is missing ($75).

From left: Art Deco lines, marked "Old English Sampler," lion, H&K, made in England, similar petit-point patterns used by many manufacturers, c1920 ($120); Alfred Meakin, mark has name and crown, "England," delicate pattern formed in porcelain, hand-painted detail ($85).

Larger and small versions of the same shape, by Ellgreave, many shapes and decorations made, black and red mark "A Div. of Wood & Sons, Ralph, Moses, Enoch," lions and shield, "Ellgreave, England" impressed in bottom (large pot $65, smaller pot $45).

Breakfast set with only teapot and cup, marked "Ye Olde English Grosvenor china, Jackson & Gosling, England," cup marked "Aynsley, England, Bone China," with crown and banner, c1930, slight damage ($75 for set).

Minton China, England, Haddon Hall pattern, made since 1940s, color display of flowers, note the shape of the spout which would pour without dripping ($125). (photo courtesy of Gary Stotsky, Pennsylvania)

Teapot lamp in background, no mark, gold decoration similar to items made in Japan, but could also be German porcelain, hairline crack where spout is attached ($95); chocolate pot in middle has cabbage roses, mark is "Germany" in a circle ($75); sugar and creamer are similar pattern with same mark ($65 for set).

Floral Teapots

ITEM	VALUE
Americana, large pinkish red rose, bud finial, porcelain, Japan, distributed by Enesco	$75.00-$95.00
Blue bird and blossoms, 2-3 cup, marked "Shelley, England"	$130.00-$150.00
Bright red flowers, bud finial, pottery, marked "Italy," c1950s-1960s	$45.00-$60.00
Chintz, brass bail handle with porcelain, no mark, English style	$95.00-$125.00
Chintz, distributed by Victoria Magazine, Welbeck pattern, marked "Royal Winton," modern	$150.00
Cuckoo bird, spray of wildflowers, London shape, marked "Wedgwood, Williamsburg"	$200.00
Delphinium, chintz style, porcelain, blue background, red and yellow flowers, marked "England"	$95.00-$125.00
Desert Rose pattern, bud finial, marked "Franciscan" in an arch, last made 1951	$110.00
Floral spray on bone china, white round shape, marked "England," modern	$35.00
Hand-painted dogwood, two rings form finial, German blanks, porcelain, painted, c1940s	$85.00
Heavenly Rose, scalloped edge, swirl handle, similar to RS Prussia, Japan, distributed by Enesco	$150.00
Magnolia and forsythia, porcelain attached bail handle, heavy gold, marked with crown, England	$95.00-$125.00
Magnolias, china teapot, hand-painted design, Japan, distributed by Enesco	$75.00-$95.00
Metropolitan Museum of Art reproduction, Staffordshire, England, floral, modern	$75.00
Months of the Year, birthday teapots, with flowers, 3-in. high, Sadler, England	$25.00
Multi-colored spray of flowers, 6 cup, marked "H-O-Co., Best Bone China, England," c1960	$95.00
Old Country Roses, a Royal Albert pattern with gold trim, by Royal Doulton, modern	$125.00-$150.00
Rose chintz pattern, large cabbage rose, creamware, by Johnson Bros. for Wedgwood	$100.00
Scalloped edge, swirl finial, pink around top, similar to RS Prussia, marked with raised star	$135.00-$150.00
Summer Chintz pattern, stoneware, marked "Johnson Brothers," modern	$85.00
Violet chintz, scalloped edge (see Heavenly Rose above), Japan, distributed by Enesco	$140.00
Violets, stacking cozy set, round bodies, violet finial, Japan, distributed by Enesco	$95.00-$125.00
Violets, swirl-shaped body, gold trim, Japan, distributed by Enesco	$45.00-$65.00

Glass
Teapots

The fragile nature of glass would seem unsuitable as a material for steeping a pot of tea. At one time this may have been true, but when the Corning Glass Works of Corning, NY, came up with a formula for glass bakeware, things changed. The first piece of glass bakeware was marketed in 1915. Ten years later, teapots were introduced.

In many ways, glass teapots are an ideal teapot. Their wonderful transparent qualities allow a person to actually view the tea brewing and stop the process at precisely the desired strength. Depending on the formula used and the thickness, glass teapots are quite durable, especially those made for stove-top use on gas burners.

While glass teapots have not been produced in the same quantities that porcelain and pottery styles were, many companies, such as Corning, saw the potential for such a vessel. Others offering glass teapots include Sears with a whistling teakettle as part of its Flamex Glass Cookware, or a teapot with a locking lid in its Maid of Honor line. The Glassbake and Fry companies marketed their glass teapots during the 1930s and 1940s. An ad from the Beaver Valley Glass Co. in Rochester, PA, shows a lovely glass teapot with etched flowers. The ad also states that this company was operated by the H.C. Fry Glass Co.

An estate auction ad from 1989 shows a collection of Foval glass teapots which have jade colored handles and finials. Part of this collection is a tea set on a glass tray including the teapot, creamer, sugar and cup and saucer. The glass has a milky tone and is not the typical clear crystal of glass teapots.

One of the dilemmas with glass teapots is the ability to identify the manufacturer, if it is not marked. The study of new glass may help determine if you've found a vintage piece, but, unfortunately, reproductions have been made of almost

Classic shape, no strainer, paper label made in Korea, modern ($35); tea bagger, for brewing tea for one with a tea bag, marked on metal frame and on bottom of glass "Tekoe Teabagger by Ekco, Made in U.S.A.," patent numbers ($25); Pyrex, Flameware line, range top model, marked on bottom, "6-cup, Pyrex, Made in U.S.A.," c1950s ($75).

every type of glass in the last half of the 20th century. On the positive side, companies, like Pyrex, etched their name into teapots, and you may be able to date it by studying the way they used their marks over the years. A great way to identify Corning glass teapots is with reprinted advertising, some of which can be found in the reference guide, *Pyrex by Corning: A Collector's Guide* (see Reference Section).

Glass teapots made to actually brew tea were made in clear or crystal, but children's tea sets were produced in primary colors by the Akro Agate company (see Children's Section for listings).

Modern glass teapots have been produced, and the most popular one is from Germany called the Jena. Listed in many mail order catalogs and available in tea or houseware shops, it comes with a glass infuser and its own warming stand. Another style is a round, globe-style pot with an infuser that lifts the tea out of the brew with a push of the plunger.

Vintage glass teapots are becoming harder to find, especially those in perfect condition. The spout of a glass teapot is prone to chipping as is the underside of the lid. Collectors should purchase glass teapots even with some damage, as long as the price has been adjusted, until they can locate better examples. Doing so may also be to your advantage in identifying another glass teapot in the future.

Glass teapots may not be as showy on a display shelf as some of your other teapots, but you can enhance their appearance by filling with any

Pyrex with etched flower design, marked on bottom with company name, under lid "Corning, Pyrex, made in U.S.A.," late-1930s into 1940s ($150 in excellent condition, $65 with spout damage); table tea, pitcher part of children's tea set ($22); colorful and imaginative individual glass project, marked with Deanna Jacobsen, 1980 ($45).

variety of interesting materials. Try some of these ideas to fill your clear teapot:

◆ Foam peanuts used for shipping
◆ Mylar tissue or crinkly ribbon used for stuffing gift bags
◆ Pastel colored cotton balls
◆ Use Stick-Um and silk flowers for a small floral arrangement inside the pot
◆ Put colored paper through a shredder and scrunch to fill
◆ Batting used to fill pillows
◆ Lightweight or plastic colored beads

Collectors need to be aware of new glass teapots bearing price tags in amounts like their 1930s counterparts. Glass teapots from Taiwan or China will be more apt to have bubbles or imperfections in the body and the finishing touches will be less defined. An example is the cutting or filing of an edge rather than the crafted rolled edge either along the top of the teapot or end of the spout.

Glass teapots are a wonderful visual aid when used to illustrate how to brew tea or capture the image of tea time and have been used frequently with recent articles. These pots are clearly the choice demonstration tool when passing along the method for brewing a perfect pot of tea. Showing off the amber-brown warmth of a pot of tea, glass teapots will provide a transparent tea time view.

Glass Teapots

ITEM	VALUE
Bodum teapot, strainer, plunger stops brewing process, two sizes, modern	$25.00-$35.00
Floral arrangement inside non-functional pot, attached to wooden base, modern	$28.00
Germany, designer Wilhelm Wagenfeld, infuser included, modern	$75.00
Jena teapot, warming stand, glass infuser, made in Germany, modern	$75.00
Pyrex, round shape, blown glass handle, marked "Pyrex, USA," c1930s-1940s	$110.00-$125.00
Pyrex, squat shape, blown glass handle, c1925-1940, marked "Pyrex, USA"	$125.00
Shield, initials and floral sprays engraved on body, bird finial, unusual piece	$650.00+
Working movement inside glass teapot, cat on swing, marketed by Enesco	$35.00

Graniteware Teapots

Graniteware was made from the late-1800s to the present, with heaviest production from about 1900 into the 1930s. Graniteware or enamelware is the coating of metal with an enamel surface using a heat application process. One or more coats may be applied, and it's thought that the higher the number of coats of enamel, the stronger the process. This may be true but other factors also account for strength and durability. How the enamel was applied, the temperature of heat being used and the quality of the enamel are all important.

The terms "graniteware" and "enamelware" are basically interchangeable. Most antiques and collectibles sources refer to this colorful product as graniteware. The Sears, Roebuck and Co. catalog of 1900 (and for many years), advertised its graniteware "True Blue Enameled Steel Ware."

Graniteware is sometimes referred to as agate ware and this may have been the result of marketing in a certain area by the Manning Bowman catalog which touted its "pearl agateware." As with many antiques or collectibles, certain terms vary by location and are influenced by the manufacturer or marketing methods.

Some graniteware is referred to as porcelain especially in regards to larger items such as advertising signs or kitchen table tops. Hoosier cabinets are an example—they often had a porcelain work top and storage bins. This material is basically the same as enamel or graniteware but may be a thicker application.

Graniteware implies the granite-type design or swirled pattern often associated with this product, but solid colors were produced frequently. Sears' True Blue enamelware was a blue and white swirl pattern with solid white on the inside. Sears also boasted "four coats of the finest grade of enamel

From left: Small, frog motif, hand-decorated enamel over brass, paper label "Made in China," modern, $25; cat motif, hand-decorated enamel over brass, paper label "Made in China," modern, $25. Many shapes and themes made of this type enamel ware.

are applied on both inside and outside." Sears offered a wide variety of items including a teapot and a tea kettle.

While most kitchen utensils were completely coated with enamel, other items, such as teapots, were a combination of graniteware and another uncoated metal. The teapot lid was often left as a polished, uncoated metal, such as pewter, enhancing the look and practical appeal. Hinged lids were a preventative invention for those that have a tendency to fall off when pouring tea and subsequent breaking or chipping. Graniteware teapots with hinged lids were made both in enamel and uncoated metal. If the lid was uncoated, the handle and spout were fashioned to match.

Other variations of graniteware included an attached wood handle in either a curved or straight shape. Teapots with an enamel section in the handle are harder to find. Combination metal-and-enamel body teapots are highly sought after among collectors.

The metal bodies of graniteware teapots were often made by one company and then the enameling and finish work done by another. Stamping companies fashioned metal to certain specifications, even for graniteware production.

Certain colors are more predominant than others. One of the most common colors is the blue marbled or swirled. The blue can range from cobalt to a pastel blue and any variation in-between. The next most-used color was gray, again in a wide range of shades but usually blended with black or a darker gray rather than the white swirl. Collectors specialize in certain colors such as red marble variations, which are hard to find. Other colors or styles that collectors especially watch for are multi-colored patterns, those with floral or decaled decorations and rare colors, such as pink.

From left: Brown/red small size, hinged lid, minor chips, printed mark "Albert Pick & Company, Chicago, Czechoslovakia," c1930 ($55); bell shape, wicker handle, marked "Japan" and symbol, no chips or wear, 1960s ($45); brown, lid has locking prong, minor wear, no mark, c1930s ($45).

Graniteware was made in several countries and the easiest teapots to locate will be those made in America. Unfortunately for collectors, enamelware was marked more often with paper labels than with a permanent mark, making it difficult to determine the manufacturer without some research. Collectors can reference two well-documented books on graniteware by author Helen Greguire (see the Resources Section).

Some of the more popular American manufacturers include the Manning, Bowman & Company, Nesco Royal Granite Enameled Ware, Central Stamping Co., Lalance & Grosjean Manufacturing Co., Granite Ironware, Lisk or Lisk-Savory Ware, Vollrath and United States Stamping Co. There are many more companies which produced or marketed graniteware. Some were only in production for a few years while others have a long history and thus their items are more plentiful. Some graniteware was produced to be sold with enameled stoves and marketed as such.

Graniteware was also made in Canada, Germany, Czechoslovakia, Poland and England. The Elite Company exported its graniteware to the United States and this name can be found with either Austria or Czechoslovakia.

Because graniteware does chip, teapots in mint condition are a special find and the value will reflect their condition. Prices given in this section assume there will be slight wear or chipping but this shouldn't detract from the teapot when displayed. Large, unsightly chips should devalue the teapot about 25%.

Graniteware is increasingly hard to find. Many major decorating and collectible magazines have featured this colorful collectible, raising the awareness of collectors. If this early American-style teapot attracts your attention, should you find one with an affordable price, you won't regret the purchase. Because of graniteware's colorful country charm, they're snapped up fast and appreciate quickly.

Graniteware with metal trim and hinged lid, hand-painted floral design, teapot given as a wedding gift in 1898, no mark, possibly made by the Manning Bowman Company, some wear, chip on inside ($225).

TEA NOTES

Large teapot with pewter handle, lid and spout, made by Manning, Bowman & Company, no mark but shown in an ad of 1876, called Perfection Granite Ironware (ad states: Silver and Nickel Plate, Rolled Britannia, Planished Copper and Tin Ware, Factories: West Meriden, Connecticut, Salesroom: New York). Value ($325).

January is National Hot Tea Month

Tea Council of the U.S.A. invites everyone to join the pleasures of tea with its annual National Hot Tea Month during January. Whether drinking tea to relax or for its many health benefits, Americans are enjoying an unprecedented demand for all kinds of tea with tea consumption more than doubling from 1990 to 1996, and this trend is expected to continue into the 21st century.

Take time for a cup of your favorite tea, either in a local shop or a steamy pot at home. Not sure what kind of tea you'd like? Try a black tea brewed lightly—start by brewing for a shorter period than recommended on the package. A bit of sugar or honey and milk will bring out tea's best flavor. Morning tea drinkers favor Earl Grey, which is flavored with oil of bergamot. Darjeeling blends are great for afternoons. Love the flavor of tea in Oriental restaurants? Try green teas. And join Americans consuming almost 50 billion cups of tea per year.

From left: Paneled teal green design, marked "Germany," many chips and wear around spout, handle and lid, c1930 ($30); traditional round shape with applied decoration, chipping around spout and underside of lid, marked "Rd. No.," dating pot from 1904-1905, made in England ($75).

Graniteware Teapots

ITEM	VALUE
Avocado green, modern fruit motif, distributed by J.M. Fields, c1970	$45.00
Blue and white mottled, individual, wooden handle, marked "Manning Bowman Quality"	$125.00
Blue and white mottled, white inside, mark includes lion and pot, possibly German	$95.00-$120.00
Blue Willow, large 10-cup size, no mark, c1940s-1950s	$75.00-$95.00
Blue, robin's egg blue, 4 cup, no mark, some wear around hinged lid and rim, c1950	$50.00
Brown, large 6-8 cups, no mark, USA or Japan, large chip	$35.00
Brown, orange and blue air-brush look, leaves and flowers, 4-cup, marked Elite	$85.00
Cherries or flowers, children's set, set with 6 places, European, c1890-1920, wear	$350.00-$425.00
Gray mottled, white metal upper with engraved Oriental scene, Manning & Bowman	$225.00
Gray, dark mottled tone, individual size, marked "Made in Romania," modern	$30.00
Green, grayish tone, tangerine inside, marked "Vollrath Ware, Sheboygan Wis.," c1960	$100.00
Pewter trimmed, white enamel souvenir of Oakland, individual size, rare	$500.00
Pewter trimmed, white enamel with castle scene, hinged lid, large 8-10 cups	$395.00
Red, deep color with curved wooden handle, hinged lid, marked Germany with lion and teapot	$250.00
Red, individual size, polka-dot, hinged lid, marked "Made in Czechoslovakia"	$75.00
White, hinged lid, 4-cup size, marked on side "Savory Ware by Lisk-Savory, N.Y."	$85.00-$95.00

Holiday Teapots

Left: This antique reproduction doll belonged to author's grandmother; the doll is holding A Cup of Christmas Tea miniature tea set, made in China, distributed by Waldman House Press. The set is valued at $30. The blown glass antique teapot ornament on tree was made in Poland ($25).

ost holiday teapots cross into the figural category out of necessity in portraying a particular theme. In direct relationship to the popularity of a particular holiday is the number of teapots created for that theme. Christmas teapots take the lead in both availability and desirability, although teapots have been produced for almost every other holiday, including birthdays.

Not all holiday teapots are figurals, especially porcelain and china pots created for a special Christmas tea time or part of Christmas dinnerware lines. The popularity of a simple story written by Tom Hegg in 1982, *A Cup of Christmas Tea*, has spawned a whole line of items to have your own Christmas tea. The 6-cup teapot was first made in 1992, but other matching pieces include a cup and saucer, tree ornaments, teaspoons, a miniature tea set and napkin rings. These items are made in Taiwan and marketed by Waldman House in tea shops and mail order catalogs.

While records show a Father Christmas teapot made by Sadler in the 1930s, the popularity of holiday themed pots gained momentum in the 1950s. Christmas teapots may be as simple as a pottery

Above: Holiday Hide-a-way, battery operated, musical tea pot house lights up and figures move around the table, made in China, 1992, marketed through House of Lloyd and Christmas Around the World ($85).

pot with applied decals of holly or Santa. Or they can be as elaborate as a moving teapot marketed through the House of Lloyd's "Christmas Around the World" catalog. This battery-operated teapot plays music, lights up and has moving figures inside a resin teapot called "Holiday Hideaway."

Rabbits and bunnies make for natural teapot shapes with their lopping ears ready to form a spout or handle. Many represent Easter and springtime, while others were J135

ural teapots of this furry form. Bunny teapots can be found in a variety of poses from sitting, holding a carrot or two bunnies doing the tango. A wonderful pottery bunny teapot was made by Sylvac, England, in the late-1930s and early-1940s, available in several pastel shades. Sadler produced a very similar bunny teapot.

A very realistic rabbit teapot was made by Royal Doulton called "Bunnykins," c1940. Hand-painted detail on this pot is almost real enough to reach out and pet.

The Fitz & Floyd company has produced many holiday teapots in the last 20 years with the majority for Christmas but other celebrations are represented by teapots such as the Statue of Liberty in 1995 and a patriotic decorated Whitehouse teapot

Bunny with bundle of carrots, modern porcelain, backstamp "WCL," paper sticker "Made in China" ($22); bunnies dancing, modern porcelain, backstamp "Lillian Vernon, Virginia Beach, VA," made in Taiwan ($28).

Bunny with hat, large teapot made in U.S.A. and marked "Treasure Craft," modern ($40).

in 1993. Several teapots have been designed in the shape of hearts to celebrate Valentine's Day, including one with an arrow projected through it by Rising Hawk in the early-1970s. Turkey teapots in various styles, pumpkins and jack-o-lanterns and even wedding cake teapots have been fashioned in recent years. A teapot can be found for almost any special occasion or holiday but they will be predominantly from modern manufacturers.

In this category, collectors won't find as many vintage teapots, but should watch for those made from a durable porcelain and plenty of hand-painted detail. Many holiday teapots made in the Orient have been marketed, which are low quality porcelain and chip or crack easily. The original price was quite low and secondary prices should

From left: Heart shape with bow for finial, modern, porcelain, marked "Lillian Vernon," Taiwan ($18); pincushion, thimble sits on spout, I Love You message, modern, no mark ($12); Tea for Two, stacking pot and two cups, white porcelain, modern, no mark ($22).

Celebrate the 4th of July with this patriotic teapot, no mark, made in Japan, wicker handle ($50).

be valued respectively, although they do have collector appeal. If these teapots were only marked with paper labels which have been removed, they will be hard to identify.

Holiday teapots by well-known manufacturers such as Fitz & Floyd, Russ Berrie or marketed by Enesco will increase in value and are normally of high quality. Each year, more holiday teapots flood the retail market to the point where you could have themed collections within your collection representing all of your favorite celebrations.

From left: Santa petting dog, modern, Home for the Holidays, made in China ($25); dog and cat in sleigh, modern, Home for the Holidays, made in China ($25).

From left: Christmas tree shape, large, modern, Taiwan ($15); Snowbear in Santa's sack, painted over glaze, modern ($18).

From left: Sango, Silent Night pattern, c1980, Japan ($125); village scene, Russ, c1980, Taiwan ($30).

From left: Hand-painted over white porcelain, mark, made in Italy ($35); Christmas tree shape, small, modern, China ($12); small pottery, holly leaves, Crawford Pottery, Dayton OH, c1950 ($20).

From left: Roasting chestnuts scene, Sadler, made in England, Christmas Holiday ($35); Cottage Christmas, Ron Gordon Designs, 1988, Taiwan ($25).

From left: Small, resin teaset, cottage shapes, modern ($14); wooden teapot house, lid opens to hold set, Midwest Importers, China ($15); resin teaset, Christmas tree-shape with bears, modern, China ($16).

From left: Potpourri burner, carolers, Taiwan ($15); lighted cottage with snowman, Midwest Importers, China ($25); Blue teapot, small, with snowman, stars and moon, made in Taiwan ($12).

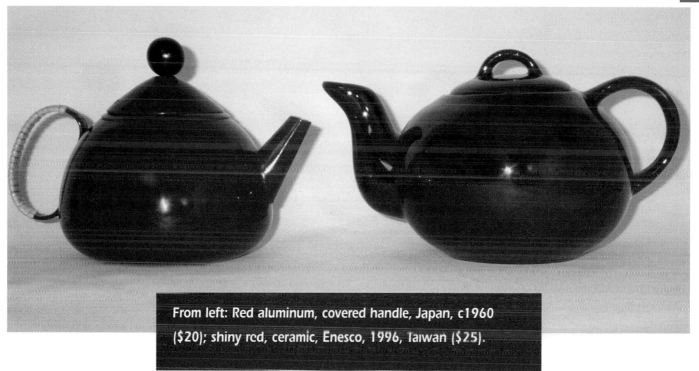

From left: Red aluminum, covered handle, Japan, c1960 ($20); shiny red, ceramic, Enesco, 1996, Taiwan ($25).

The book A Cup of Christmas Tea has inspired a whole line of china tea ware, including full-size and doll-size tea sets, teapot napkin ring in foreground, resin ornaments shaped like artwork from book were made—even a teaspoon with this holly motif is available. Teapot made in China, distributed by Waldman House Press. Teapot ($65); cup and saucer ($35); sugar and creamer ($30).

Christmas Tree decorated with teapot shaped ornaments: Hallmark, Enesco, hand-blown from Germany, Poland and Japan, ceramic, resin and wooden are some examples. Collectors can decorate a whole tree with the available teapot ornaments.

From left: Santa Solo, stacking teapot and cup, hand-painted, Cardinal, Inc., China ($22); Nutcracker, Russ, c1980, China ($30).

From left: Snowman, pottery, blue scarf, hand-made ceramics, 1969 ($28); elf, paper sticker on side "Golden Crown, E&R, Western Germany," backstamp on bottom also reads "Western Germany" ($85).

Large teapot house is electrical decoration, animated Santa pops out of top while bears move inside, plays various Christmas tunes, steam waifs from spout, by Mr. Christmas (available at Sears) made in China, 1998 ($50).

Holiday Teapots

ITEM	VALUE
Bear holding a candy cane, one paw is spout, marked "Made in Korea," by Fitz & Floyd	$75.00
Father Christmas, hand-painted detail, pottery, marked "Sadler," c1930s-1940s	$150.00
Festive mouse climbs out of Santa's sack, porcelain, Omnibus, Taiwan, modern	$55.00
Happy Holidays or Christmas Time pattern, Christmas tree design, marked Nikko, Japan	$75.00
Holly Ribbons pattern, fine bone china, marked Royal Worcester with lion, unicorn, modern	$185.00
Peppermint twist shape, candy cane handle, marketed by Dept. 56, modern	$30.00
Poinsettia and ribbons trim white porcelain, marked "Japan," modern	$30.00
Poinsettia, large flower with greens on fine bone china, marked "Made in England," modern	$45.00
Pursuit dinnerware pattern, hounds and hunters, semi-porcelain, marked "Noritake, Japan"	$95.00
Santa popping out of chimney, Santa is lid, marked "Carlton Ware," c1980	$65.00
Santa holding a cup, marked "Made in Taiwan," modern	$25.00
Snowman, hand-painted ceramic, distributed by Dept. 56, modern	$40.00
Snowman, holds broom & snowball, hat is lid, marked "Made in Korea," by Fitz & Floyd	$75.00
Teapot shape, star finial, white porcelain, greetings on base, marked "Wade, England"	$85.00

Individual-Size Teapots

hether at home, in a restaurant or at the office, one or two cups of tea are all that is usually desired by an individual. There's something odd about trying to make half a pot of tea, so individual-sized pots make perfect sense. This individual size originated with the earliest Yixing teapots from China where tradition encouraged small amounts of the enticing tea. A single pot of tea is brewed for each person so that everyone receives the best tea.

An individual teapot with a cup that stacked together has been marketed since the 1980s and can still be found in mail order catalogs or tea shops. Made of porcelain or china, variations on this "Tea for One" allow for continued interest with individuals only wanting a "spot" of tea. In ceramic classes, "Tea for One" has been a favorite to decorate yourself and then have it glazed and fired.

When using individual-size teapots there are some slight differences in steeping. Because of their smaller size, tea may not need to steep nearly as long as a 6-cup teapot. Many individual-size teapots do not have the strainer and were devised for use with tea bags rather than loose tea. A separate infuser or strainer could be used to brew loose tea and the amount of tea leaves decreased. When using this smaller sized pot, realize that you will get an initial cup of tea and then only enough to warm it up. If you normally desire more tea, you may want to go with a regular size pot rather than an individual teapot.

Individual-sized teapots have been used for decades on trains, ocean liners and in restaurants. These pots were made from heavy porcelain to withstand the rigors of daily use and the bumping or clattering that may occur. Collectors should

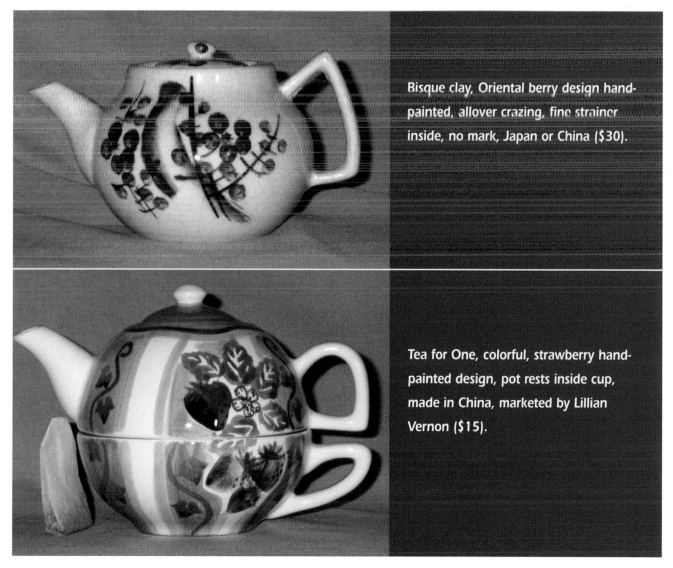

Bisque clay, Oriental berry design hand-painted, allover crazing, fine strainer inside, no mark, Japan or China ($30).

Tea for One, colorful, strawberry hand-painted design, pot rests inside cup, made in China, marketed by Lillian Vernon ($15).

watch for these smaller pots with the business's name applied either on the side of the pot or underneath. Individual-size cube-shaped teapots originated for use on ocean liners where they could be stacked for convenience and safety. Produced by companies in England, the United States and Japan, their novel shape has also been utilized for restaurants and personal use.

Cube teapots were patented in Britain and early registry marks date from 1922. These square teapots were made with accompanying pieces, such as a creamer, sugar and coffee pot, which fit onto a tray with indentations to keep them from sliding. Many are marked with the company that originally purchased them such as a brown-glazed cube stating: "Los Angeles Steamship Company, The Cube, British Patent No's and Reg.'d No's…Made by George Clews & Co. Ltd., Tunstall, England, supplied by Stonier & Co., Ltd., Liverpool."

Hall China produced cube teapots under British

Front, from left: Cube, recessed lid, brown glaze, marked Los Angeles Steamship Co., George Clews & Co. ($45); cube, knob finial, fluer-de-lis decorations, modern, marked "Royal Crownford, England" ($30); back, from left: cube, handle on side, recessed lid, hand-painted decorations, marked "Made in Japan" ($25); cube, recessed lid, marked "Hall China," made under British patents, Nos. on mark ($30).

Cube, pink with Art Deco designs, marked "Made in Japan" ($30). (photo courtesy of Gary Stotsky, Pennsylvania)

trademarks and patents which are marked on their pots along with their name. U.S. patents were also secured, and these teapots have all of this detail in the mark along with, "Cube Teapots, Ltd., Leicester." While these teapots are no longer used for commercial purposes, they make wonderful individual teapots or just a novel attraction in your collection.

Railroadania enthusiasts enjoy a myriad of once commercially used individual teapots. Collectors have identified more than 45 pottery and porcelain companies that produced teapots over the years from the plain and simple to highly decal-decorated, including railroad logos. Many of their shapes were similar; if a backstamp is missing, they may be hard to identify. An example is a pair of teapots which set onto a recessed tray with one pot intended for tea, the other for hot water. Hall China and the Buffalo China Company produced comparable sets, although decoration or glazes differed.

A small number of railroad teapots were the 4- to 6-cup size, but the majority were individual size. Some designers incorporated a metal hinged lid and a metal handle. Other styles include a recessed lid which allowed them to be stacked for storage. Afternoon tea was offered on many rail-

roads with a special menu for this occasion. Collectors are finding railroad teapots harder to find with increased interest in this selective area. Highly desired are those pots with more detailed decoration and ample marking or backstamps to be able to trace their history.

Individual-size teapots are perfect for serving tea in a restaurant and many of the same U.S. companies have produced teapots for a variety of commercial businesses. Many restaurants still use the heavy porcelain teapots although more and more are turning to either metal or plastic teapots. As with the railroads, when a restaurant goes out of business, the supplies are sold off. Items permanently marked with the establishment's name and/or logo are usually not suitable for use by another business and end up on the secondary market for collectors. These teapots generally do not carry high price tags but can be an addition to your collection with a bit of history behind them. If unknown, don't hesitate to ask the seller about where an individual teapot may have originally been used. Sometimes only the name of the establishment is marked, but you may be able to find out the city or town and the era in which it was used.

Individual-size teapots are great as promotional

Front left: Restaurant ware, marked "Jackson China, 1961, New York State Property, A.L. Cahn & Sons, New York"; front right: Hall China, silver spout, restaurant style, marked "Stakups by Hall"; back: bright floral, marked "Made in Czechoslovakia," c1930.

items and this has been practiced to some degree ever since tea was shipped in crates from China to Europe in the late-1600s and early-1700s. Small Chinese teapots were packed within these crates of tea to the chagrin of European potters who had yet to produce a hard-paste porcelain.

Promotional and premium giveaways have long been a salesman's friend. The method of offering something extra for the sale of regular products was the driving force behind a very successful business begun in 1875 by John D. Larkin—The Larkin Soap Company. While this company marketed soap and other home products from 1875-1960s, it offered many premiums, especially china and pottery items. In 1903, Larkin's Buffalo Pottery opened in New York, and premiums included teapots and tea sets, among other semi-vitreous porcelain items. Since Larkin's slow decline in the mid-20th century, Buffalo China (renamed in 1956 and a subsidiary of Oneida Ltd.) has produced many individual-sized teapots for commercial and advertising purposes.

Other U.S. names to watch for on individual teapots include Fraunfelter (or Ohio Pottery Co.), Homer Laughlin, Shenango China Co., Syracuse China Co., Porcelier and Jackson China. British pottery, porcelain and china companies have produced many individual-size teapots with an emphasis on breakfast sets. These sets have become quite pricey in recent years, and collectors watch for complete sets which vary in the number of pieces offered. A common breakfast set includes the teapot, sugar, creamer, cup and saucer and a toast rack set on a tray. Chintz-decorated breakfast sets can be priced as high as $300 (when they include extras such as the toast rack). Other breakfast sets are simply the teapot, sugar and creamer on a tray, and the cup and saucer may or may not have been offered.

Individual-size teapots present tea time for one person or served in bed on a tray while collectors enjoy their smaller dimensions, making them easier to display. You will find other examples of individual-size teapots throughout this book, but a varied selection is presented here.

From left: Petite roses decorate porcelain, marked "Vitreous" on basket, Edwin M. Knowles China Co., patented, c1930 ($45); shell designed set, china, sticker "Made in Romania" ($40 for set).

From left: Brown coralene, gold decor, marked "Made in Japan," c1950 ($22); brown glazed, coralene decoration, "Made in Japan" backstamp and raised in pottery, some wear in the gold, c1950 ($20).

From left: Pottery, brown, lid recessed, marked made in U.S.A. ($25); brown lustre, "Made in Occupied Japan" raised mark on bottom ($35).

From left: Ming Tea Co., mark includes "Hartford Conn., Made in Japan, EPI Curio No. 112" ($25); Ming Tea Co., marked includes "Hartford Conn.," paper label increases value, states tea type ($32).

Front left: Brown lustre, marked raised on bottom, "Sadler, Made in England," c1930 ($25); front right: stacking set, painted over glaze, sticker "Made in Japan," c1950 ($22); back: blue porcelain, no mark, possibly U.S.A., c1940 ($28).

Front left: Porcelain, tiny roses, Gibsons, Staffordshire, England, crown mark, c1960 ($28); front right: pottery, pink, marked "Ford" with a cross through oval, c1950 ($20); back: chocolate brown lustre, square shape, raised mark "Made in Japan," 1929 ($30).

Two colors of the Salada Tea teapot, pottery, marked "Salada, U.S.A.," note the S-shaped finial, possibly made by the Nelson McCoy Pottery, 1930s, ($30 each).

Miniature sized Cadogan teapots from left: brown pottery, mouse on top of pot, China backstamp ($28); blue glazed pottery, fine detail with applied decoration, no mark, possibly made in China ($30).

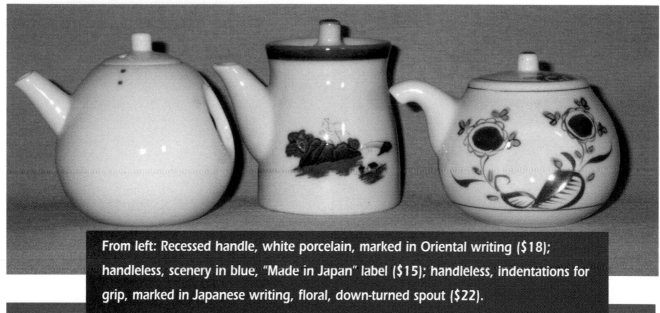

From left: Recessed handle, white porcelain, marked in Oriental writing ($18); handleless, scenery in blue, "Made in Japan" label ($15); handleless, indentations for grip, marked in Japanese writing, floral, down-turned spout ($22).

From left: Large cozy covered pot, white pottery, felt-lined copper cozy, no mark ($28); cozy covered, white porcelain, felt-lined copper cozy, raised "Japan" mark on bottom ($25).

From left: Dragonflies, hand-painted design over-all, marked in Chinese writing ($22); Japan, pottery, heavy glaze decoration, no mark, hand-painted flowers and leaves ($15); cloisonné-look with overall decoration in glaze, marked "Made in China" with Chinese writing ($22).

Individual-Size Teapots

ITEM	VALUE
Copper lustre, band of white and copper poppies, Wade, England, 4-in. high, marked	$45.00
California Poppy, ATSF Railroad china, marked "OPC, by Syracuse China, U.S.A.," c1947	$65.00
Porcelain with metal lid, handle, for Golden Rocket RR, Chicago, Hall China, c1952	$75.00
Queen Anne breakfast, teapot, tray, cup, sugar and creamer, Royal Winton, England	$500.00
Russet brown, green and gold detail, by Nancy Lamb, Iron Mountain Potteries, 1977	$50.00
Tea for Me, green scroll design, pot stacks into cup, marked "Made in England," modern	$60.00
Tea for One, cup fits upside down on pot, marked "Bing and Grondahl, Scandinavia," 1977	$45.00
Tea for One, pot stacks on cup, country heart motif, made in China, modern	$15.00
Tricolator Product, Carraway shape, Hall China.	$30.00
Twin tea, two pots, hot water and tea, on tray, many decorations, Hall China, c1930	$75.00

Miniature Teapots

$\mathcal{M}$iniature teapots are purely whimsical and satisfy our fascination with anything produced on a tiny scale. Steeping or pouring tea would be impossible for these tiniest of teapots. Most miniature teapots or tea sets were produced since the late-1800s when production methods allowed for better control in pottery, porcelain and china processes.

Not only is the small scale amazing when you come across a tiny teapot, but the detail of the decoration on some teapots is beyond belief. Other miniature teapots have hand-applied decoration or gold trim that makes one wonder how it could ever have been done. Today, factories use free-standing magnifying glasses to aid workers doing minute detail. Most miniature teapots were more likely hand-painted with the naked eye.

Miniature teapots predominantly mimic their larger counterparts, such as the Blue Willow pattern, copper teapots, the Chinese cylindrical shape, Wedgwood jasperware or Limoge china. Japanese china teapots with wicker or rattan handles have been produced in miniature. During the Occupied Japan period, tiny floral sets on trays were plentiful.

Miniature teapots have been produced in almost every medium including silver, silverplate, glass, pottery, china, pewter and wood. Using ingenuity, for a period in the late-1950s and into the 1960s, tiny teapots and other items were fashioned from peach pits as souvenir items.

The tiniest recorded teapot is a gold fingernail charm—the kind which are attached to your fingernail when receiving a manicure. For teapots that stand alone, the smallest teapot is only 1/4-inch high and is a painted metal, probably made for miniature enthusiasts furnishing their doll house or shadow box. Other amazingly tiny teapots are only 1/2-inch high and made out of glass, pewter, copper and porcelain. There are miniature teapots only 3/4-inch high and some wonderful examples include a glazed blue pottery, a speckled graniteware, Santa with matching creamer and sugar, an early American style in silver and a pewter set on a tray.

While miniature teapots have been made for decades and became popular after World War II, during the 1970s through the 1990s craft stores with miniature sections and shops specializing in miniatures have grown in number. This has generated an abundance of tiny teapots produced mainly in Japan, China and Taiwan. Some of these are of high quality materials and hand-painted, while others are crude white metal or plastic.

One of the problems for collectors of miniature teapots is the fact that most are almost too small to have manufacturer marks and are difficult to identify. As with larger teapots, getting to know the different styles, painted decoration and so on, can help identify the origin.

Because of their size, tiny teapots don't usually carry a very high price tag. Most can be purchased

Snowman, Cardew Designs, made in England, 4-in. high ($30); Keystone Cop, Artone, marked with palette, 4-in. high ($25).

Three tiny Paul Cardew teapots from a series of 12, Old Black Stove, Kitchen Sink and Baking Day, packaged in boxes imitating tea crates, made in Devon, England, 1994 ($25 each).

for less than $20, with the average around $10. Exceptions occur when purchasing teapots that are 1-1/2 to 3-inches high, made by porcelain or china companies such as Wedgwood or figurals by Cardew. Modern tiny tea sets range from $20-$60, depending on the pieces and style.

One of the latest trends is collecting all of the shapes from designers such as Paul Cardew. His line of figurals features pieces of furniture and appliances found in the home and so many have been made that a mini home could be completely furnished. One series of Cardew miniatures issued in 1994 offered 12 different teapots. Other companies have offered similar small teapots, priced reasonably from $12-$30. Other designers offering figurals have prices as high as $89, such as Swineside Ceramic's Victorian bath series with a mini claw-foot tub.

A popular category with collectors are the miniature resin tea sets. These sets come in a variety of themes that could either be figural or just a popular design. Collectors should purchase only resin sets of high quality manufacture. Look for smooth edges and undersides, hand-painted detail that is within the design and removable lids. Some of the finer resin tea sets are made in the United States and will be marked or hand-signed. Examples of resin tea sets include a sunflower motif, hummingbirds and flowers and figural teddy bears having

tea. Hundreds of designs have been produced in almost any imaginable theme at prices ranging from $16-$25. Resin tea sets will not appreciate as quickly as porcelain or china tea sets, although some collectors specialize in these interesting miniatures.

Collectors should be aware of any tiny teapots being passed off as vintage when they are really reproductions of older pots. An example is new floral teapots made in Japan, about 2 inches high, which have a pattern similar to those made in the 1940s and 1950s. Most Japanese teapots of that era were marked with red or black backstamps; those with no mark or a gold paper label may be modern. An oval label with a blue background and white text of "Japan" was used from the late-1950s-1960s on miniatures large enough to affix. The problem is that paper labels do not always stay intact or may even have been removed. Older Japanese miniatures usually had some of the bisque porcelain unglazed either on the bottom or sometimes even the inside was left unglazed.

A current miniatures collecting category is porcelain boxes that open with a clasp and are hinged. Examples with either teapots molded on top or those in the shape of a teapot can be found in gift shops and mail order catalogs. Porcelain boxes were first marketed by a Limoge, France company. Prices are expensive, starting at just under

From left: Wood base, mouse house of resin, removable lid, no mark, paper sticker removed ($22); wood base, mouse house of resin, removable lid, no mark, paper sticker removed ($22).

$100 and ranging into the hundreds of dollars. Other companies have seen the potential for this collectible on a more affordable scale and versions have been made in England and Taiwan. Prices can start as low as $12 and average $22 or higher, depending on the hand-painted detail or where they were made.

When collecting miniature teapots you'll always be able to find room for one or two more because of their convenient tiny size. Collectors may want to use tiny dabs of "Quake Hold" or Stick-Um material to keep mini teapots in their place. I use this method to place tiny pots along the edge of my computer allowing me to enjoy the little reminders of tea time whether I'm writing or surfing the Internet.

From left: Limoge, France, cobalt, tall shape, 2-in. high, marked Limoge ($20); Limoge, France, teapot on warmer, candlestick inside, 3-in. high, marked, with building ($28); Limoge, France, London-style in light blue, Victorian scene ($20).

Top, from left: Yixing styling, shaped like a rabbit ($12); Banko styling, applied-slip decoration, reed handle, marked in Japanese lettering ($25); tiny clay teapot, no mark ($12); bottom, from left: Yixing-style, metal bail handle, impressed design, chop mark under button size lid ($25); two miniature Yixing style teapots from clay, no markings, center right has Yixing-style, applied decoration, no mark, 2-in. high ($30).

From left: Violets, bamboo handle, no mark, Japan, bisque china ($25); squat-shaped, floral, bamboo handle, marked "Japan," 3-in. to handle ($22); squat-shaped, floral, bamboo handle, 4-in. to handle, marked "RPC, Kyoto, Japan" ($28).

Various shapes and styles of brass teapots, made in India, some marked, etching more desirable, values range from $12 to $15.

Back, from left: Copper, top half decorated, souvenir, no mark ($10); small copper pot, on stand, bail handle with holder, no mark ($15); copper, kettle-style, hinged bail handle, no mark, 3-in. high ($15); front, from left: brass, tiny, solid body, no mark, 1-in. to handle ($10); copper and brass, Art Deco-style, marked "Made in England" ($18); brass, copper bottom, no mark ($15).

Top: miniature brass teapots, first one has solid body, no marks any ($12 each); bottom: copper, ribbed body, marked Italy, 1-1/2-in. high ($15); shiny copper pot with no mark, bail handle ($12); low-style, Art Deco, marked "England" ($15).

Silverplated, kettle-style, wooden handle, marked "Schade," Italy, 3-1/2-in. high ($20); pewter, no mark, common shape for modern miniature teapots ($12); brass, bail handle, wood finial, marked "Japan" ($15).

Bottom: Miniature tea set marked "Made in Occupied Japan," square shape typical of that era ($25); top: tea time clock miniature, marked "Made in Occupied Japan," square shape ($22).

From left: Porcelain, ivy leaves hand-painted, no mark, 2-3/4-in. high ($12); Germany, applied flowers and Dresden-type decoration, "Germany" in double circle ($30); Germany, applied flowers and Dresden-type decoration, no mark, 2-1/2-in. high ($28).

Plastic tea set from Dime Store, no mark, packaged, from Japan ($10); plastic tea set, white on tray, with package (not shown), c1960, original price was 10 cents, Japan ($18).

Three blown glass teapots which are often found at craft fairs and county fairs, painted details on each (miniature glass teapots normally have no markings) ($3.50-$5 retail or $6-$8 on the secondary market.)

Peking duck on stand, removable lid, bail handle, China, 2-in. high ($25); mini teapot with bowl and saucer, modern, made in China, teapot 1-in. high to handle ($12); scene hand-painted set of teapot, cups, platter, made in China ($22).

From left: Bone china, hand-painted flowers, blue-green trim, no mark, 3-in. high to handle ($25); bone china, applied and hand-painted flowers, intricately woven wicker handle, no mark ($25); bone china, hand-painted flowers, wicker handle, ribbed shape, no mark, 3-1/2-in. ($25).

Plastic painted teapot, uncertain whether part of set or was a charm ($8); plastic, elephant, pink and blue, part of set, marked "Made in Hong Kong," c1960s ($12); window shade pull, plastic, flower decal, no mark ($15).

From left: Carrot, porcelain, hand-painted details, made in Thailand, 2-in. high ($18); pumpkin, mini, applied detail of leaves and flower, no mark, 1-in. high ($15); hamburger on plate, porcelain, no mark, hand-painted details, 1-1/2-in. high ($14).

From left: Blue lustre, applied flowers, marked "Made in Germany" in circle ($25); windmill scene, hand-painted design, marked "Made in Japan" ($20); lustre, common scene with house, marked "Japan," c1950, 2-3/4-in. high ($18).

From left: Blue and white rooster, modern, marked China ($15); string holder with rooster motif, open in back to place ball of string, marked paper label, Japan ($22); restaurant china, chicken design, marked "Chowning's Tavern, Williamsburg, Virginia" ($28).

Four small, Victorian styled teapots, similar to Limoge miniatures, no mark, modern ($12 each); trinket box, tea set on top, hinged, modern, 1-1/2-in. high ($10); cloisonné, multi-colored, on wooden stand, no mark, made in China ($25); tall pot with hand-painted flowers, marked "Japan," c1930s ($22).

From left: Heavy green glaze over white porcelain, no mark, possibly Japanese and part of a set ($15); elephant, pottery, glazed, no mark, no painted detail ($15); blue glaze over porcelain, no mark, styled after U.S. pottery ($20).

From left: Celadon-colored pot with bird detail, marked "Made in China" ($15); elephant, blue and white design, no mark, made in China, 2-1/2-in. high ($18); blue and white porcelain, modern, paper sticker removed, possibly made in China ($15).

Three examples of blue and white designs which are popular with collectors. All three are marked "Made in China," modern ($15 each).

From left: Wooden, reed for handle, solid pine ($15); wooden, bail handle, no mark, 2 1/2-in. to handle ($15); dark wood, removable lid, no mark ($12).

From left: Tea set with hand-applied decoration, on tray, no mark, made in Japan, possibly during occupied period ($28); bail handle of attached porcelain, modern, marked "Mason's Chartreuse, England" ($20).

From left: Applied flowers and hand-painted decoration, marked "Made in Occupied Japan" ($25); applied flowers to top of this gift-style teapot, modern, marked "Sandford, Fine Bone China, Made in England" ($20); bone china, gold trim, hand-painted flowers, kettle-style, marked "France," 3-in. high ($28).

From left: Glass, colored detail, open bottom, no mark 1-1/2-in. high ($8); glass, strawberry or other decal, no mark, 3-1/2-in. high ($12); glass, on glass tile, no mark, worn coloring, lid and body one piece ($10).

Dickens'-type character with face on each side, Artone, England, 2-in. high ($25); Toby-style, head figure, Captain, HMS, Artone, England, palette mark, 2-in. high ($25); Toby-style, head figure, Victorian gentleman, Artone, England, palette mark, 3-in. high ($25).

Clown, Artone, marked with palette, England, 3-in. high ($22); Dickens' character, marked "Artone," 2-in. high, part of series ($25); Toby-style, head figure, Palace Guard, Artone, England, palette mark, 3-in. high ($25).

Toby-style, Dickens' character, Artone, older marked with palette, England ($25); cup and saucer of Colonial man, marked "Made in Japan" ($20 for set); Toby-style, Dickens' Mr. Pickwick, Artone, marked with palette, England ($25).

Colonial man, teapot, cup and saucer, hand-painted detail, marked "Made in Japan" ($28 for set); elephant, orange lustre, man riding, part of tea set, 1932, marked "Made in Japan" ($25).

Three brass and copper teapots, kettle-style, souvenir of various places, no marks ($10 each).

Three copper and brass teapots, no markings; one on far right is souvenir from England with coat of arms, ($12-$15 each).

Silverplated, traditional-style on tray, solid pieces, no mark ($18).

Back, from left: Wedgwood, bone china, floral design with bird, marked "England," c1980 ($45); Wedgwood, black, unglazed, marked with England ($38); Front, from left: Wedgwood, Jasperware, light blue, marked "England" ($45); Wedgwood, Peter Rabbit, bone china, England, 1983 ($45).

Modern miniature teapots and sets. Only teapot on stand is marked with sticker "Made in Taiwan," miniatures such as these range from $12-$20 on secondary market, less on the retail market.

Miniature Teapots

ITEM	VALUE
Aluminum, removable lid, molded flowers, 1-1/4-in. high, no mark	$8.00
Ceramic, white with blue country heart, 3/4-in. high, no mark	$5.00
Colonial style with straight side handle, metal, painted, 3/4-in. high, marked "Japan"	$10.00
Egyptian style painting, allover design, 2-1/2-in. high, marked "Corinthian Askos by Helena"	$15.00
Floral decor on china, 3-in. high, paper label "Genuine Bone China Taiwan," c1980	$12.00
Metal, green with pink painted flowers, country style pot on a tray, 1-in. high, modern	$12.00
Metal, painted black with gold Oriental scene, bail handle, 3/4-in. high, marked "Japan"	$10.00
Metal, painted like graniteware, set with cups, pot 1-in. high, paper label "Made in Taiwan"	$10.00
Mexican dancers decal on wood, lid opens for dowel ring holder, 3-in. high, c1940s 1950s	$20.00
Milk glass, with gold trim, 1 1/4-in. high, part of set, made in Japan, no mark, c1950s-1960s	$22.00
Pewter, 3 pieces on tray, old English-style, pot 3/4-in. high, no mark (paper label missing)	$12.00
Pewter, old English style with wood-look handle, set on tray, pot 3/4-in. high, marked "Pewter"	$25.00
Pottery, smooth blue glaze, fixed lid, 3/4-in. high, no mark	$12.00
Resin, "You're Tea-rrific!" on teabag, mouse popping out, Enesco, Japan, 1990	$15.00
Resin, bird house shape, various styles, removable lid, made in Taiwan, 1-1/2-in., modern	$8.00
Resin, country cottage teapot, hand-painted, 1-1/2-in. high, label "Made in China"	$12.00
Resin, mice around house, removable lid, 3-in. high, marked "Dezine, PA," made in China, 1993	$18.00
Resin, teapot townhouse, 6-in. high, paper label, Hamilton Gifts, made in Korea, 1988	$20.00
Santa face, ceramic, hand-painted, pot 3/4-inch high with sugar & creamer, no mark.	$12.00
Sterling set on tray, Victorian-style, pot 2-in. high, marked sterling on each piece	$35.00
White metal, painted white with Blue Willow design, 3/4-in. high, no mark	$8.00

Music Box Teapots

From left: Ballerina twirls as music box plays, porcelain, paper label on music box "General Ind. New York, Made in Japan," marked on porcelain "Made in Japan," c1960 ($45); snow globe, music box, resin body, plastic base, marked "Made in China," plays "I'd Like to Teach the World to Sing," modern ($28).

*M*usic box teapots are a 20th century invention directed more for gift-giving than actual tea time, although many can be used for tea as well. These melody-producing pots have a special hollow area in the body where a music box is installed. The music box is wound and a pin mechanism allows for interruption of the actual playing. When the pot is picked up to pour tea (or just view, in the case of a novelty item) the music begins playing. Once the teapot is rested on a table, the music stops.

While music boxes were invented in the 1800s, the height of popularity for musical teapots in the United States was from the 1940s through the 1960s. Because of a renewed interest in tea time and increased collector awareness of teapots, new musical teapots have come onto the market in the 1990s.

Most music box mechanisms used in a teapot were made in Japan while the pot may be manufactured in any number of countries. This can be misleading if the teapot's mark or backstamp is concealed by the music box and the visible identification is on the music box. Others were not marked under the music box because paper stickers were common during the 1950s and 1960s.

During the 1960s, music box items, which included a twirling plastic ballerina, were popular, and a china teapot was produced with the same theme. Amazingly, even after the addition of a music box underneath and the ballerina in an alcove of the body, tea could still be made in this teapot. Inside the teapot, a piece of paper explains instructions for washing the teapot. Marking for the teapot is a gold foil label on the bottom of the music box which reads "Do not overwind, Copyright General Ind., N.Y., Made in Japan."

Since there must be some way to attach the music box to the porcelain or pottery body, several ingenious ways have been devised. One method uses small little support bars that fit into tiny notches in the pottery and are attached to the wood base of the music box by miniature screws. This can be adjusted as needed when the screw is loose, to fit slightly varying depths of the notch in the pottery. More modern designs form feet, with a hole, on the underside of the teapot where a small nut and bolt can be slipped through the porcelain and a portion of the music box. The newest music box teapots sold through The San Francisco Music Box Company, which has both stores located in malls and a mail order catalog, feature the music box anchored to a plastic base with tension-bearing clips to hold the mechanism in place. One particular floral teapot was produced by the James Sadler & Sons, Co., but it is only marked "Made for The San Francisco Music Box Company in Staffordshire, England."

From left: Yellow pottery, allover crazing, no mark, music box says "Japan," c1940 ($45); brown scenery, transfer print, porcelain, no mark, paper label "Nasco, Del Coronado, Japan," c1950s-1960s ($50).

And what tune would you expect to hear while pouring tea? You guessed it—by far the most popular is "Tea for Two," while the song "I'm a Little Teapot" is also used on occasion.

Music box teapots can be used for steeping a pot of tea while enjoying their melodious sound but care must be taken when rinsing them out or washing. The music box portion cannot get wet; if you really must immerse in water, this mechanism can be removed. It's not advisable to do so because you will run the risk of damage, usually to the portion which holds the music box in place and then it can't be re-installed. A careful rinsing with soapy water and then clear water is all that's needed should you use your music box teapot for tea time.

There are music box teapots which are purely decorative and it will be obvious that they aren't intended for making tea. Many of these have snow domes with some tea time scene inside and also play music. These have been made since the 1970s, marketed as gift items. Musical teapot snow domes don't have the same mechanism which turns the music on and off as other pots. Instead they are intended to play out the tune. Enesco has marketed various versions, usually with mice peeking out of the teapot or in playful poses—prices average $25. Others are made in China from hand-painted resin. The base is also resin with room allowed for the music box, making them heavy. Retail prices average $15 to $20. On the secondary market, prices go a little higher.

Collector's can determine the age of music boxes by the material to which the music box is attached. The oldest examples from the 1940s to late-1950s are wood. During the 1960s and into the 1970s, a fiber board material was used or a thin plywood. By the mid-1980s plastic bases were formed.

Whether a functional teapot or purely a novelty, music box teapots will add a lively note to your collection. Now I just want to know why a darling white porcelain teapot with black musical notes decorating the body does not have a music box inside.

From left: Moss Rose, panel shape, porcelain, mark in red "Made in Japan" on body, plays "Tea for Two," c1960 ($65); Moss Rose, oval shape, china, paper label on music box "Wales, Reg. U.S. Pat. Off., Made in Japan," plays "Tea for Two," c1950 ($75).

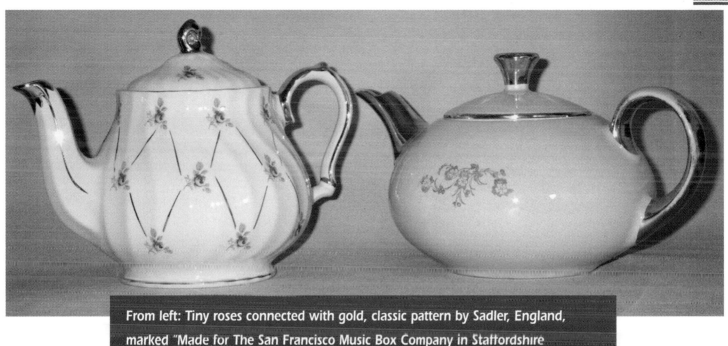

From left: Tiny roses connected with gold, classic pattern by Sadler, England, marked "Made for The San Francisco Music Box Company in Staffordshire England," plays "Tea for Two," modern ($75); yellow-glazed pottery, wear on gold trim, wood music box frame, possibly by Pearl China Co., U.S.A., c1940 ($55).

Music Box Teapots

ITEM	VALUE
Bluebird, colorful hand-painting, music box underneath, plays when lifted, Enesco	$150.00-$225.00
Colonial man and woman, lady and dress are pot, man is handle, music box marked "Japan"	$85.00-$120.00
English cottage scene, souvenir type, white porcelain, music plays when lifted, c1930	$65.00
Floral, circular handle, plays "Tea for Two," Enesco, Japan	$95.00-$135.00
White china, music plays and mice scene on lid revolves, Enesco, Japan	$45.00

Novelty Teapots

From left: Candle, graniteware look, label "Lorelei Candles, Handmade, Gatlinburg, TN" ($12); Fiesta Ware tea kettle, yellow, enamel, plastic handle and finial, mark includes name, "Copco, The Homer Laughlin China Co., Made in Taiwan" ($35); yellow candle, Fiesta Ware, Copco, Div. of Wilton Ind., made in China ($15).

The charm of novelty teapots is purely in their unique shape, since they are not intended for tea. Collectors of any subject eventually find something shaped like their collectible category only with a differing function.

Teapots are no exception, and all kinds of practical and purely whimsical items have been shaped like a teapot. They range from clocks and salt & pepper shakers in the 1940s to candles and wind chimes in the 1990s. If you enjoy teapots, there are novelty items to enhance your collection and home. Novelty teapots range in size from miniature to being too large for pouring (for the smallest of teapots, see the "Miniatures" section). This section will describe those teapots which are commonly given as gifts or are gift-store items but are beginning to show up in antique shops or country stores.

While collecting Precious Moments is a subject in itself, many teapots and related items have been produced with the design of these lovable children. Precious Moments has been dubbed "America's Hummels," and for good reason. The many designs created by Samuel J. Butcher now have a following of 300,000 club members and will only have been produced for 22 years in the year 2000.

There have been Precious Moments teapot shaped snow globes, figures having tea titled "Friendship hits the spot," teapot-shaped jewelry and even a Precious Moments teapot clock. Marketed by Enesco, some teapot-shaped items by this organization look similar to Precious Moments because they are produced with the same quality porcelain and decorated with pastel colors.

Only those items with the Precious Moments' logo are authentic and collectors need to be aware of this because of price differences. Pricing of Precious Moments depends if the item is still being produced or is retired. So far, most pieces will continually increase in value from their original retail price.

Resin figurines have flooded the market since the late-1980s, with many teapot-shaped items. Collectors need to be aware that those with wooden bases and finer detail will appreciate in value but don't expect this to happen very quickly. Many craft and specialty stores have offered resin teapot-shaped figurines which feature playful mice. One company marketing these items is Dezine, out of Pennsylvania, and its items are made in China. Resin teapot-shaped novelties are marked with paper stickers and the majority made in China, Korea and Taiwan.

Not all novelty teapots are from the last 20 years, but mass production has allowed for more

Front, from left: Enesco giftware, "I love you, Mother," paper label and backstamp, modern ($20); Precious Moments tea time, battery music box, gold label "1993 Samuel J. Butcher, Enesco, Taiwan" ($30); back: Jesco gift ware, under license from Enesco, Kewpie figure, made in China, modern ($20).

From left: Precious Moments, miniature tea set on stand, marked "1989, Samuel J. Butcher, Enesco" ($25 for set); Precious Moments tea time clock, battery operated, marked "1993, Enesco, Made in China" ($45); Precious Moments tea time napkin holder, marked "1993, Enesco, Made in China" ($38).

and more inexpensive items to flood the retail market. Brightly colored plastic teapot kitchen items from the late-1930s through the 1950s are becoming highly collectible. A spoon rest, salt & pepper holder and shade pulls are just a few of the teapot-shaped household items to be found.

Teapot-shaped items were produced in porcelain during the same era by U.S. and Japanese companies. The California Cleminsons is one U.S. company that made several teapot shaped items, such as ceramic wall pockets for plants and plaques with rhymes. The Cleminsons produced their pottery from 1941-1963. Their cheery colors are easily recognizable on hand-painted items such as a spoon rest or a plaque shaped like a teapot that says "Time for Tea." These items are usually marked with a black backstamp bearing their name which will identify their ware from some similar lookalikes, mainly made in Japan or individual porcelain projects.

During the mid- to late-1990s, many teapot-shaped photo frames were produced from a variety of materials. Teapot collectors can find their favorite shape to hold special moments made from resin, wire, pewter, and a gold-colored metal. A teapot pottery incense burner from the 1970s was produced in several glazed colors. From the 1950s to the present, teapot-shaped teabag holders have been made in porcelain, china and even plastic. Many have been decorated and sold as souvenir items while others represent popular themes through the decades. Whimsical teapot-shaped faces adorn a set of teabag holders that fit onto a storage rack, made in Japan.

Artist Mary Engelbreit has perpetuated novelty teapot items with her brightly colored teapot themes since the 1980s and her items can be found not only in retail stores but within the pages of her own magazine called Mary Engelbreit's Home Companion. Recent items include teapot-decorated tins, teapot magnets or teapot-shaped decorative ornaments meant to be hung any time of the year. Her artwork features primary colors with black backgrounds and borders and is easily recognizable. Currently, many styles of teapots are available along with all of the decorative items such as a tapestry-style pillow or tote bag with teapot designs.

Today, teapot enthusiasts will find in-store displays and specialty shops devoted to teapots, teapot-shaped items and tea time novelties. Collectors can adorn their home with teapot pillows, wall paper, curtains, a yearly calendar, fan pulls and even a terra cotta flower pot with a spout and handle ready for real or silk flowers. If your favorite teapots are vintage designs and English patterns (and you're thinking that modern novelty items are too gaudy), you'll be delighted to find these antique styles reproduced on decorative items.

Teapot-shaped tea bag holders, from left: yellow pottery with metal strainer could either strain tea from teapot or be used to place tea bag, no mark, possibly made in Japan ($35); baby bird is perched on a limb of holder, marked "1977 Mary Mugg, Licensee Enesco," red and gold Enesco sticker ($15); ceramic happy face holders say "I will hold the bag" and bow ties are 3D, allowing for standing up ($22 for set of two).

Three sets of salt & pepper shakers, all made in Japan, 1940s and 1950s, from left: Gray dragon ware set is especially collectible, marked "Made in Japan" ($22); light gray, smaller sized pots had paper label that just read "Japan" ($20); hand-painted floral and gold, marked "Japan," wear on gold ($15).

Three sets of salt & pepper shakers all made in Japan from 1940s and 1950s, from left: chrome set with red plastic handles marked "Made in Occupied Japan," shakers rest into openings on tray, some wear on chrome ($25); gold-colored metal, plastic bottom threaded to open for filling ($15); plastic bottom and metal tops on colorful shakers, finial has threaded stem, top comes off for filling ($18).

Three sets of ceramic salt & pepper shakers, all made in Japan from 1940s-1950s, from left: Orange-painted set with bail handles marked "Japan" ($20); tiny hand-painted flowers on teapot and sugar bowl set, marked "Japan" ($20); black handles on teapot and sugar bowl set, Oriental flowers, marked "Japan" ($20).

Teapot-shaped tea bag holders: Common item for souvenirs as shown by the two shown at left and right, both made in Japan ($12-$15 each); center: set of happy face tea bag holders which come with their own portable storage rack, c1950s, each a different pastel shade, marked "Made in Japan" ($25 for set).

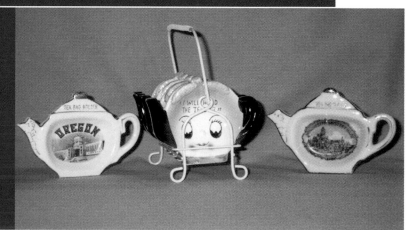

From left: Wall pocket, bail handle, opening for utensils or plant, similar to Cleminsons, "A singing kettle and a kitchen bright makes a home your hearts delight" ($35); wall pocket, "Take time for tea" hand-painted, marked "The California Cleminsons," c1950 ($40).

From left: Cookie cutter in teapot shape, Fox Run, modern ($4); room thermometer, made in U.S.A. by Tel-Tru Thermometer Co., Rochester, N.Y., c1930s-1940s ($45); cookie cutter with handle, made by Ann Clark, Ltd., U.S.A., with pamphlet, recipe ($12).

From left: Dinner bell, gift-boxed, backstamp inside bell "18K gold, decorated, Enesco, 1973" ($25); modern teapot-shaped photo frames are available in many materials: pewter, gold colored, Victorian style, decorative wire ($10-$20 each).

From left: Wall pocket, clock, c1950, no mark, similar to many U.S. pottery ware ($45); wall pocket, cup and saucer, c1950, no mark, possibly U.S. ($35).

From left: Oil lamp, miniature, china pot, no mark, made in Japan, possibly Lefton ($20); night light cottage, bisque porcelain, marked "Golden Memories, Little Dreamers, Hand-Made in Spain," 1992 ($30); oil lamp, miniature, china, no mark, made in Japan, possibly Lefton ($20).

Pair of teapot wall pockets, fruit motif, marked "Made in Japan" ($30 for pair).

Metal tray has Japanese tea ceremony utensils impressed and/or raised, no mark on interesting piece that could be a tea bag holder ($30); tea tile with teapots motif made by the Gladding McBean Pottery Company, also marked "Hermosa" and "U.S.A.," c1930 ($50).

From left: Plastic salt & pepper set rests on teapot holder, made to hang on wall, marked raised on back: "M. Stephens Mfg. Inc., L.A. Calif., Made in U.S.A." ($30); metal tea canister, painted red, bakelite handle on hinged lid, marked on bottom "Kreamer," possibly part of kitchen canister set ($25).

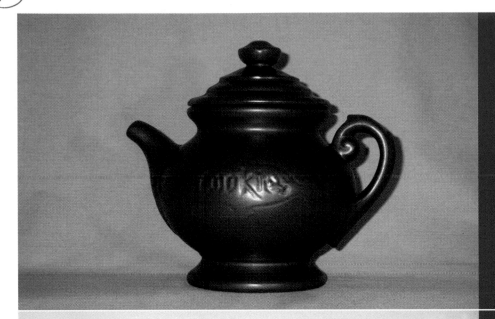

Cookie jar, matte glaze, marked "McCoy, U.S.A.," c1960 ($85).

From left: Pot pourri holder, hand-made, wood cut-out, "1993 Del Mar Fair, Calif." ($25); incense burner, glazed porcelain, no mark, 1970s ($20).

Two Avon teapots items from the 1980s, from left: Basket came with tea bags, could be used for pot pourri after tea is gone ($20); ceramic teapot is individual size and has colonial styling, came gift boxed ($28 with box).

Novelty Teapots

ITEM	VALUE
Brass, key ring holder, teapot-shape, made in China, c1985	$15.00
Candle, shaped like a Fiesta Ware teapot, yellow, modern	$15.00
Clock, pottery-shaped design like teapot, plastic back, Sessions, c1940	$85.00
Friendship, water scene, Precious Moments, girls having tea, paper label, 1990	$75.00
Greeting card holder, wooden box, teapot laminate, made in Taiwan, from Current, Inc.	$10.00
Polished aluminum trivet, teapot-shape spells TEA, sticker "Made in India," modern	$15.00
Pot pourri burner, electric, pottery, made in Taiwan, 1989	$18.00
Resin, wood base, teapot mouse house, Dezine, PA, c1990	$24.00
Soap dispenser, wood, hinged lid, for dry soap before liquid dish soap, no mark	$30.00
Teabag holder, bird scene, Mary Mugg, sticker, "Enesco, Japan," 1977	$12.00
Teapot lamp, copper pot, wood handle and base, no mark, with shade, electric, c1940	$35.00
Teapot lamp, pink porcelain, no visible mark, with shade, electric, c1950	$95.00
Tin, painted thermometer and key holder, Tel-True Therm. Co., U.S.A., c1940	$45.00
Wall pocket, tea spoon holder, wicker handle, pottery, no mark, possibly Japan	$25.00
Wind chimes, miniature, magnolia blossoms, made in China, tea cups, modern	$20.00

Teapot wall pocket and cup, hand-painted pottery, no mark, possibly Japan ($30).

*P*orcelain has changed dramatically during the 20th century, with a wide variation in the strength, feel and weight of this normally glazed medium for teapots. Most teapots produced today are some type of porcelain although the terms "porcelain" and "china" are used interchangeably to refer to a similar composition. This is understandable because china or bone china is a type of porcelain.

Porcelain, once referred to as hard-paste, was first produced in China and records point towards the T'ang Dynasty which was 618 to 906 AD. Other studies believe some of the finest porcelains in history were produced during the Sung Dynasty from 960 to 1279 AD.

Although Chinese export porcelain enticed the Europeans, it was not formulated in Europe until the early 1700s in Meissen, Germany. Later, methods were brought to England where attempts were made to formulate a hard porcelain. Josiah Wedgwood is credited with first producing porcelain in England during the late-1700s. True porcelain was not produced in America until the 20th century.

Porcelain that has been fired but not glazed is called bisque and was popular during the Victorian period. Some bisque teapots have a clear glaze on the inside of the pot to prevent the staining which would be difficult, if not impossible, to remove. Wedgwood jasperware teapots are this bisque type of porcelain although its modern teapots are not glazed on the inside. Another English company, J. Dudson of Hanley, Staffordshire, produced jasperware-style items, including teapots with a glaze on the inside. One example even has a clear, light glaze on the handle. Bisque and jasperware-style teapots have been produced by many companies both in England and Japan. The term "bisque" may also be used to refer to the unglazed portion of a porcelain teapot.

Quality porcelain teapots produced in the United States and England are often a vitreous china which is a reference to the glass content or kaolin (decomposed feldspar—aluminum silicate) in the clay. This is the ingredient which produces the hardest body and when fired at temperatures above 1,400-degrees Celsius, a white porcelain is formed.

The Hall China Company is an example of one company which has achieved success by producing a vitreous type of porcelain. In 1904, Robert Hall, son of the company founder, began searching for a method to produce a durable porcelain with only one firing. In 1911 he succeeded and this formula for porcelain has allowed for all of the wonderful Hall teapots found in most collections today. Hall China is still in operation with restaurant and promotional items a mainstay of its production, although many of its teapots have been reproduced in different colors or decoration than vintage pots of the same pattern. New or old, Hall China teapots have never ceased being enjoyed for steeping tea or collecting. This vitreous china doesn't craze, is not easily chipped and withstands the rigors of boiling water for tea.

Another American pottery, with a shorter history but similar success with vitreous porcelain production, is the Porcelier Company. Many types and styles of teapots were manufactured by this company from the late-1920s to its closing in 1954. Today, collectors desire these pots of relatively large

From left: Floral spray on multi-sided white porcelain, label made in Japan, c1980 ($28); Frank Lloyd Wright, Art Deco design, 1994, marked "Copco, Art Institute of Chicago, Made in Philippines," attached tag ($55).

size, made of an off-white porcelain. Their durability has allowed for practical tea brewing and has kept them attainable for collectors today. Porcelier is marked with the company's name and the term "vitreous china." The firm also marketed many styles of drip coffee pots with an aluminum section for the grounds. Collectors need to be aware that many times the drip section is removed and then they resemble teapots.

While porcelain teapots are some of the best suited for steeping a pot of tea, crazing is often a problem. Crazing is the hair-line cracks in the glaze which can be on the inside of a pot, on the outside, or both. This can occur for many reasons. It might even originate in the kiln because the body and glaze have different rates of expansion and contraction when exposed to extreme heat or cooling. While this crackling effect may even be caused purposely by some manufacturers, the majority would not have allowed such a piece out of the factory. Heat or cold in storage or shipment can cause crazing. The most common cause is the very purpose a teapot was intended for: adding boiling water to the pot. Preheating the pot with warm water can help prevent crazing. The only cure is to have the perfect recipe for porcelain ingredients and the right temperature which will cause the glaze and body to bond together. Preheating a porcelain teapot can prohibit a certain amount of crazing, but I've seen pots continue to become crazed even after warming the pot. High-quality porcelain-producing companies in Japan, China, England, other European countries and the United States have labored to create a porcelain that will withstand the test of time and repeated use. Other companies use a body or paste that produces a temperamental teapot with the fragility almost like soft-paste porcelain (although true soft-paste porcelain is no longer made).

Much of these wares have come out of Japan, Taiwan, China and Malaysia.

Collectors should be aware of a reproduction (see page 173) which has shown up in 1998 and 1999 and has even reached the secondary market of unknowing dealers and buyers alike. This porcelain has a celadon colored background and a blue design mimicking flow blue or an old transfer ware. The mark on these teapots and other items is a shield with a lion and unicorn on either side and the words Victoria, Ironstone. Two quite similar marks have appeared: on one, the animals are filled in and Victoria may or may not appear. On the other, the backstamp has more of an open look. This backstamp is a reproduced variation of the British Royal Coat of Arms mark, used by more than 50 companies in the United States and England during the late-1800s and early-1900s. The unglazed portion on the bottom of these reproductions has been stained black to look old but a closer look reveals an evenly distributed staining rarely occurring in real use. The scene on this reproduction is of a town square with a center tower and figures both on horses and walking. A catalog in which pieces of this ware were offered states that they are "Reproduced from original, 19th century English designs." While they may make nice country accents, beware of vintage prices attached to such porcelain reproductions.

While not a reproduction, Blue Willow decorated items have been made by many porcelain companies almost since it's inception during the 1700s. You can purchase new Blue Willow items but collectors need to study the marks, the type of porcelain or pottery to know what they're buying. If you're not sure a teapot is authentic, don't buy it until you're able to do some research or unless the price is low enough—under $30.

From left: Blue and white, similar to Blue Willow but actually called Spode's Tower, mark includes pattern name, "Copeland, England," London-shaped pot, c1910 ($85); Blue Willow pattern, no mark, possibly U.S., this pattern still being produced by some companies ($45).

From left: Glossy black and gold, marked "Hand-Painted, Warranted 22k Gold, Made in U.S.A.," unknown maker ($40); smooth lines on black glaze, paper label and mark impressed on bottom, label says "Bay Keramik, Free of Lead, Dishwasher Safe," in several languages, c1970 ($45).

Brown and yellow mottled pattern, note the interesting style to handle, backstamp "Victoria, Porelite, Czechoslovakia," also decal mark ($75 for set).

From left: Pearlescent lustre and gold, marked "Sadler, England" with banner and crown mark ($45); beautiful swirling pattern on this teapot made in China, mark includes Chinese lettering, note the handle with plenty of room to grip ($35).

Black-glazed porcelain set from Guam, side handle pot, 5 cups nest in their own box, gold bird design, no mark ($45).

From left: Silver lustre, octagon shape, marked "Sutherland, Made in England," c1930 ($85); Art Deco concentric lines, backstamp Price Bros., impressed "Streamline [pattern name], Made in England," c1930 ($75).

From left: TeaMaster, made by Hall China, marketed by the Twin Spout Pottery Co., c1940, yellow glaze ($95); applied flowers, decorated like a wedding cake, individual ceramics project, hand-painted detail, no mark ($75).

From left: Speckled glaze, marked "Portmeirion, Meridian Susan Williams-Ellis, Made in England," c1962-present ($65); grayish-white, unglazed, inside and handle have clear glaze, marked "Argyle, J. Dudson, Hanley," c1888-1898, some damage to spout, made in England ($85).

From left: Metropolitan shape by Franciscan, from its Tiempo dinnerware line in "mustard" color, c1940s-1950s ($75); white satin glaze on this Franciscan shape in its Coronado Table Ware, made from 1936-1956, marked is "Franciscan Ware, Made in California, U.S.A.," also marked under lid ($75).

From left: Hall China, Boston shape, marked in gold and impressed, Hall China 6-cup, U.S.A. ($40); magnolia flower, marked "Harker, Royal Gadroon, Oldest Pottery in America, est. 1840" ($45).

From left: Mickey Mouse and Donald Duck enjoy coffee, bought at Disneyland, mark with star, "Crafted with Pride in U.S.A., Treasure Craft," modern ($30); apple tree design is called "Orchard," marked "Wade, England," c1980 ($40).

From left: Pony Express Rider, part of a series called Historical American, designed by Joseph Boggs Beale, about 19 scenes made from late-1940s to 1950s, porcelain, Homer Laughlin China Co. ($85); white fruit pattern, marked "Egg Shell Theme, Homer Laughlin, Made in U.S.A." and wreath, this company is still in production in Newell, WV ($75).

From left: Small porcelain teapot with black musical notes, no music box, marked "House of Prill," shield, modern ($28); "A Proper Cup of Tea" directions are printed on this pot with whimsical red and black motif of cows, stars and moon, porcelain, marked "Boston Warehouse for the New Basics," 1990, Workman Publishing, made in Japan ($30).

From left: Dripless spout, locking lid, marked "Swinnertons, Staffordshire, England, Patented" ($40); Johnson Brothers, Rosedawn pattern, England ($65).

1950s pink speckled pots: one on left is not marked, pot on the right marked "Monterey, Made in California" with state outline, California pottery has seen special interest in last decade of 20th century (left $35, right $65).

From left: Orange lustre, square shape, marked "Crooksville, China Co.," c1940s ($75); celadon, Hall China Victorian line, marked "Hall" in circle, c1940s ($60).

Two Sadler teapots, from left—from Minster series, this pot is titled "Fighting the Spanish Armada, 1588" with descriptions on the bottom, Sadler's crown and banner mark, "Made in England," modern ($40); country blue rings decorate this Sadler pot, marked raised name and "Made in England," c1960 ($35).

Booths Real Old Willow by Royal Doulton, from its Majestic Line of tableware, 1981, England ($85). (photo courtesy of Gary Stotsky, Pennsylvania)

Circular shaped teapot, Victorian scene, no mark, hand-painted and gold decoration, Limoge, France, modern ($55).

Hall China teapot, Star pattern, made in 1930s-1940s, gold decoration ($65).

Winfield, marked "True Porcelain, Winfield, Hand Crafted China, Made in U.S.A.," late-1940s-1950s, crack in handle ($30).

True Friendship is described poetically on this octagonal shape, made in England ($65).

Hall China black teapot with silver glazed spout, made and used especially for famous restaurant in New York City, 21 Club ($85). (photo courtesy of Gary Stotsky, Pennsylvania)

Nantucket basket pattern, holds 3 cups, Wedgwood, made exclusively for sale at Murchees Tea in Canada ($95). (photo courtesy of Gary Stotsky, Pennsylvania)

Celadon-colored pitcher that mimics flow blue and blue transfer ware. This reproduction is being sold as antique because of the older-looking style. Many different pieces have been produced, including a teapot.

The British Coat of Arms has been used to formulate a mark on the bottom of this reproduction, although it doesn't state where it was made. The only words are "Victoria" and "Ironstone." Even the bottom of this piece has been blackened to pass it off as antique.

Modern teapot with country scene has pretty mark on bottom "Our Home, National Housewares by David Davir, Japan, ($25). Ribbed body and heavy glaze on oval shaped pot by Fraunfelter Pottery Co., mark also includes "Ohio" in diamond, lid is ill-fitted, same shape used for Lipton teapots, c1930 ($55).

Three Japanese teapots with side handles—bottom, from left: Applied coralene decoration, apple blossom, intricate strainer inside, red impressed mark in Japanese on underside near handle ($45); swirled colors of pottery so thin it's like porcelain, marked in Japanese under handle ($45); top: part of set with covered cups, flying turkey design, marked in Japanese, bought in Sasebo, Japan, 1970s ($55 for set).

BREW YOUR TEA THE TEA MASTER WAY

1 — Pre-heat the pot by filling it completely with hot water and letting it stand for a couple of minutes before emptying.

2 — Put three good teaspoonsful of tea leaves or the equivalent in teabags into the tea compartment which has the large opening.

3 — Fill both compartments with fresh boiling bubbling water to within about ½" from the small overflow hole in the partition as seen under the cover.

4 — Let the brew steep from 3 to 5 minutes so that it will have tang and aroma.

Before serving the tea please notice the small ringlike mark on the handle which indicates the tea side. Remember that only properly brewed tea can be diluted without impairing the flavor.

Tea Masters can also be used for any other two liquid combinations, if not filled to its full capacity.

Tea Masters come in 10 beautiful pastel shades: canary, ivory, turquoise, cobalt and marine blue, maroon, emerald, black and brown which are also available in a gold decoration and our special Chinese red.

Twinspout Pottery Co. Inc.

1616 LURTING AVE.   NEW YORK 61, N. Y.
WESTCHESTER 7-4620

TEA *to your* TASTE *with* TEA MASTER

REG. U. S. PAT. OFF.

A VITRIFIED CHINA *Combination* TEA *and* HOT WATER POT
BUILT TO HOLD THE HEAT AND TO SERVE TEA AT IT'S BEST

With this most practical and unique Twin-Compartment teapot you may serve tea any strength desired by your guests and family.

Tea of your favorite blend is poured from one spout and by a slight turn of the hand, hot water is poured from the other spout, thereby serving tea to your taste.

Tea Master provides a practical and convenient way of serving tea without overcrowding your tray or table with extra hot water jugs. Tea Master has been scientifically designed for heat-retaining, and perfect performance, so as to brew and serve tea at its best.

Ideal for meal-time — afternoon tea — porch serving and midnight snack.

Tea Master model 44, capacity seven cups, shown serving tea.

THIS SIDE SERVES TEA

Oval Model No. 40 — 6 cup Tea Master
Beautifully glazed in many gay colors.

Tea Master model 44, shown serving hot water from the other spout.

THIS SIDE SERVES WATER

Makes an excitingly different gift for any occasion.

This pamphlet came with Tea Master double-spout teapots, made by Hall China Company and marketed by the Twinspout Pottery Co., in the 1940s. Two styles were made, one round and one oval. See pages 12 and 200 for examples of this teapot.

LONGPORT, STAFFORDSHIRE, ENGLAND

An "ARTHUR WOOD" Teapot

FOR THE CONNOISSEUR

An English teapot, backed by nearly a century of experience, which will make tea to satisfy the most discerning palate.

INSTRUCTIONS

Warm the pot, put in the tea and add boiling water. Brew for three minutes before using.

Front and back of tag from an Arthur Wood teapot, made in England, includes directions for making tea. This tag was tied to the handle of the teapot. See teapot on page 95 for example.

Porcelain Teapots

ITEM	VALUE
Blue and white, ships at sea, white octagon-shape body, marked "China," modern	$45.00
Butterfly Garden Trellis, majolica style, marketed by Enesco, marked "Japan." c1970	$50.00
Franklin Mint, repros from Victoria & Albert Museum, 1987, 12 designs, each	$75.00
Gray, blue trim in straight shape, part of dinnerware line, marked "P&C, Poland," c1960s	$45.00
Haldon's Blue Ribbon pottery, ceramic majolica style, marked "Haldon's," modern	$40.00
Individual size, restaurant ware, white, marked "Chefsware, USA"	$22.00
Ivy vines around off-white body, 10-cup size, marked "Italy," modern	$38.00
King's Arms Tavern, part of dinnerware set, royal coat of arms decor, marked "England"	$75.00
Porcelier, ivory heavy porcelain, floral spray, marked "Vitreous Hand Decorated," c1935	$75.00
Scenario, Art Deco design, black dots, designer Barbara Brenner, marked "Rosenthal"	$300.00
Spirit of tealime, teapots with sayings, floral, white porcelain, Royal Crownford, England	$65.00
Spode, Chinese rose pattern, classic shape, marked "Spode," made in England, modern	$150.00
Spode, Woodland pattern, brown floral trim, wildlife scene, deer, marked "England"	$175.00
Squared pear shape, heavy porcelain, marked "Samson Bridgwood & Son, Eng.," 1885	$135.00
Strawberry pattern on basic round shape, durable porcelain, marked "Made in England"	$45.00
Tiger stripe, round body teapot, Oriental manufacturer, modern	$45.00
Worcester, yellow background, peacock bird in center, flower finial, late-1700s	$5,000.00

Pottery Teapots

Pottery is the most widely used material for producing teapots because the main ingredient, earthen clay, is found all over the world. Clay is easily shaped or molded into an endless variety of forms where spouts and handles can easily be added. Once it has been fired or baked, clay is a durable substance for vessels of many sorts, including our favorite teapots. Most clay teapots have a glaze added either before firing or for a second firing process.

The terms "pottery" and "earthenware" are used synonymously because the clay that is used has been dug or excavated from the earth. The finer earthenware clays have a high level of iron and this will help determine the color after firing. Stoneware is another type of pottery which has less iron and the final colors are more gray and black.

Earthen clay has been a medium for utilitarian purposes since Biblical times. It's still a pliable and easily worked form today. The period when pottery teapots were first made is uncertain but before tea was ever steeped in a pot, celadon ewers in this exact form had been made in Korea. These Korean Koryo forms are from the 12th century and were fashioned for royalty. Ewers with a fitted lid, curved spout, and attached handle easily allowed for adding and pouring of a liquid. Some of these ewers are ribbed like a melon or have overall relief decoration, such as bamboo and leaves or the multi-petal lotus flower.

During the 12th through the 14th centuries, there is evidence of trade between China and Korea. In 1975, a sunken 14th century Chinese ship was discovered off the Korean coast that was filled with ceramics. Viewing these teapot-styled ewers, one can see the direct influence of Korean celadon ware on Chinese ceramics. While theories may exist about Chinese wine vessels being the first teapots, the Koryo celadon was produced in a teapot shape long before tea was steeped in a pot.

Chinese Yixing teapots, an earthenware material, were being produced by the 16th century and there is obvious influence from earlier Korean celadon. Korean potters not only influenced the Chinese but also their neighbors to the East — Japan. Celadon pottery and porcelain has been produced by all three of these countries at various times throughout history and this soft, blue-green color is still a favorite for teapots in many shapes and sizes.

While pottery and earthenware processes were well perfected by the time teapots reached Europe, a tin-glazed earthenware was produced in several countries, becoming known as Delft. The soft-paste body of Delftware never proved to be durable enough for teapots.

Some of the most highly collected pottery in England came from the Rockingham Pottery, first produced about 1750 on the estate of the Marquis of Rockingham in Yorkshire, England. Several potters occupied this estate and the famous mottled-brown color associated with Rockingham was introduced by the Brameld Brothers. Many styles and sizes of teapots were produced with this glaze, and they are very appealing to collectors today.

From left: Wheat motif on turned glaze, marked "Hand Craft, Craftsman China, Japan," 1960s ($35); black glaze, Lilly of the Valley motif, unusually large lid, no mark, paper label removed, made in Japan, c1950s ($38).

In America, two famous potteries are associated with the town of Bennington, VT. Captain John Norton founded the Norton pottery in the late-1700s where he and his descendants ran this business for more than 100 years producing all sorts of pottery including teapots, many of which were glazed in the Rockingham style. Christopher Webber Fenton, an in-law descendant of Norton, ran one of the Bennington potteries during the mid-1800s, also producing Rockingham style ware such as mottled brown teapots.

Collectors today often use the terms "Rockingham" and "Bennington" as general terms to describe a medium to heavy pottery with a brown glaze but similar wares were produced by many companies in England and the United States A teapot often referred to as "Rockingham," and a favorite with collectors is Rebekah at the Well. Although made in the Rockingham-style, it was never produced at the Bennington pottery. Taken from the Biblical story, these teapots have varying designs in relief of Rebekah standing near a well. Some designs also include this teapot's name and unfortunately, the majority have not been marked. Three known potteries (possibly more) in England and seven known in the United States, with mention of about 10-12 others in Ohio alone, produced a Rebekah at the Well teapot. At least one example was made in Japan. These teapots are the heavy pottery and brown glaze with an inherent problem on most of a lid which easily falls off. Antique shops across the country have examples of this teapot with either no lid or an ill-matched substitute lid.

The matter of origin has been debated but credit usually goes to the Edwin Bennett pottery of Baltimore who imitated an idea from cream pitchers made in England with this same design by the S. Alcock company in Staffordshire. Prices range from $45 for those without a lid to $125 for those with a lid. Because of age and use, Rebekah teapots in excellent condition are difficult to find and those with a mark will command anywhere from $200-$600.

The Barge teapot was also decorated with a brown glaze and was produced by English companies during the late-1800s into the 20th century. These are large teapots, intended as gifts or souvenirs, with a teapot finial and an inscribed area for personal messages such as "Home Sweet Home" or a birth dedication such as "William Knight, born 15, Nov. 1878." Prices vary with decoration, style and those with dates are higher in value, often into the thousands of dollars.

Some of the pottery teapots from the 1700s and 1800s were not marked, but there are sources to help in identification. Names to watch for include Wheildon, Wedgwood (producing stoneware and creamware), Minton, Chelsea and Bow. Teapots from these companies are predominantly in museums and public collections but it's possible to have examples appear in auction houses such as Sotheby's or Christie's.

Collectors are more likely to find pottery teapots from English companies established in the 1800s or early-1990s with names such as ALB (Alcock, Lindley & Bloore), Beswick, J. Dudson, Gibson & Sons, Lindgard, James Sadler & Sons, Woods &

From left: Transfer-printed design, hand-painted detail, pewter lid, Greek-type scene, marked "H.W. & Co.," wreath, England, late-1800s ($225); dessert cup and saucer, hand-painted scene, marked "Nippon" ($45); black coralene decoration, hinged metal lid and bottom plate, marked "Alexandria Pottery, Manning Bowman, Burslem, England" ($150).

Sons, Ellgreave, Price Bros. or Price Kensington, Arthur Wood and H.J. Wood. All of these companies have produced hundreds of teapot shapes and styles during the last century and while their teapots are by no means rare or highly unusual, they are quite collectible; values range from $45-$100+ depending on the pot (check the "Reference Section" for sources on identifying your English pottery teapots).

There are also some wonderful books recently available regarding marks on pottery teapots made in America. With increased awareness of U.S. pottery companies and their values comes a collectibility that has made many well-known pottery items increasingly harder to find. Teapots made by Weller, Roseville, Hull, Shawnee, Red Wing and Brush McCoy continue to rise to unprecedented prices while becoming scarce for all but the most experienced collector or dealer.

Teapots produced by lesser-known American companies are the best bet for new collectors or those with average budgets. As the secondary market taps out of certain pottery names, others will increase in value. Some names to watch for: Harker Pottery Co., Frankoma, Paden City Pottery, Fraunfelter, McCoy, Sebring Pottery, Metlox and Weil Ware. Many other pottery teapots made in the United States are well worth adding to your collection because American pottery has gained an increased appreciation since the 1980s.

Quality pottery teapots made in Japan are readily available, affordable and can add another dimension to your collecting. With a little research you may be surprised to find your Japanese pottery teapot is older than you think. A square-shaped teapot in a brown lustre was made during 1920s and 1930s. Teapots with an over-all bumpy texture and wicker or attached handles were made in Japan as early as 1916 and into the 1930s. This style was dubbed "buff sharkskin" and can be found in dark brown to a light tan color. Some styles have applied coralene or slip decoration but the majority are not marked.

Spurred by the popularity and collectibility of items made from the 1940s through the 1970s, during the last two decades of the 20th century the interest in teapots made in Japan has increased. Brown glazed pottery teapots made in Japan from dark or terra cotta earthenware and with a coralene decoration are prevalent on the secondary market. A wide variety of shapes, sizes and colors were produced between the late-1920s and the 1950s, including a cobalt hue. The majority are marked with either Japan or Made in Japan and recognizable for their white, orange and sometimes blue green dots (coralene). Brown coralene teapots were made with high quality craftsmanship in many cases, while others are crude, having pock marks or unevenness in the glaze. Prices should reflect these differences in quality.

Coralene-decorated teapots were first made in England at the end of the 19th century and well into the 20th century. Companies like Gibsons & Sons and the Alexandra Pottery Company in Burslem produced teapots with these applied enamel dots. This method was also used to decorate teapots in an effort to raise funds for World War II. Brown glazed teapots whose lids state "For England and Democracy" with tea inside were exported by the Royal Navy or Allied Fleets. The bottom marking includes a Staffordshire knot with a Union Jack, Lion and "World War II, Escorted to U.S.A. by Royal Navy." Some of these teapots have the impressed mark of "Made in England." Because a glaze was applied, this mark is sometimes hard to decipher. Thousands were made and are easily found, especially in certain areas of the country. The average price for a World War II teapot in excellent condition is $45.

One of the problems with coralene decorated teapots is that the applied dots or similar decoration is easily chipped off in use. Prices should reflect this type of wear but collectors need to realize it's quite common. The majority are also decorated with gold trim whether they were made in England or Japan. I'd be glad to buy a teapot with tea inside for any war effort, wouldn't you?

Lustred earthenware by Tobias Harrison, England, 1980s ($85). (photo courtesy of Abacus Colour Printers, Ltd., Cumbria, England)

WHO'S COMING TO TEA—
BROWN BETTY OR STANLEY WHITE?

Essentials for brewing the perfect pot of tea require a round, globe shaped teapot. This type of teapot will allow the tea to steep evenly and stay warm longer than other interesting shapes. The most common of these round teapots are brown glazed and sometimes have two or three colored bands around the top.

These brown teapots have been referred to as "Brown Bettys" for untold years and the origin of the term is sketchy. It's possible that is was first used in North America during the 1940s by importers who needed a description of this common English teapot. This name seemed to stick and it was even used in advertising to describe these practical brown teapots.

The name "Rockingham" has been applied to all sorts of brown English and American made teapots. The pottery which was established in the late-1700s on the Rockingham estate produced wonderful "Brown China." This included teapots with a reddish brown or chocolate glaze. Genuine Rockingham was no longer produced after the factory closed in 1842. Over the years, many potteries have attempted to produce teapots in the Rockingham-style, but none can compare. It's possible that the name Brown Betty was formed to some degree from Rockingham Brown china.

According to Webster's Dictionary, a Brown Betty is also the name for a baked pudding of apples, bread crumbs and spices. This sounds like a dish that could have easily been served with tea. It's possible the name of the dish came to be used for the teapot when both were used together.

If the brown teapot has a name, why not the white one? White teapots in the familiar round shape have been advertised as "Stanley" or "Stanley White." Today, globe-shaped teapots are marketed in a wide range of colors. The James Sadler & Sons Co., offers both the brown and white teapots in three sizes called "Globe White and Rockingham." Several English companies produce Brown Bettys with colored bands. Names to watch for include Gibsons & Sons, Ridgeway and A.L.B.

Brown Betty teapots are perfect to use everyday for your favorite pot of tea because they are made of sturdy pottery or porcelain and a durable glaze. Many have a locking lid and a dripless spout. The choice is up to you—will you have Brown Betty or Stanley White come to tea?

Autumn yellow on a warming stand, marked "Frankoma, Made in U.S.A.," this glaze was discontinued in 1990, c1985 ($75).

Yixing teapot, with padded storage box, fixed bail handle, allover Chinese writing, imported by Midwest Importers, made in China, pamphlet explaining "made in centuries' old tradition," modern ($75).

Vernon Kiln's Sherwood pattern, made in U.S., fall leaves are perfect for autumn table motif, marked "Vernon, U.S.A." (tea pot $35, sugar & creamer $28 for set)

From left: Riviera, by Homer Laughlin, c1950, yellow, no mark, square shape ($110); fruit motif, bright decorations, elaborate, marked "Harker, Hotoven, Oldest Pottery in America" ($35).

From left: Flower finial, knobby design, with tea tile, crazing, glazed bisque marked "Made in Japan" ($48); half-circle Deco shape, crazing, glazed bisque, crude, marked "Made in Japan" ($25).

From left: Octagon shape, floral, marked "Maruhan Ware, Japan," no lid ($12); elephant and flowers, flower finial, mouse opposite side, marked "Made in Japan" ($30).

From left: Tutti-Fruitti, basket style, Wade, England, 1990-1992, marked in mold ($30); flower finial, majolica-style, Royal Falcon Ware, June pattern, England ($30).

From left: Dark brown lustre, coralene decoration, marked "Gibsons & Sons," crown and ribbon, England, registry mark dating for 1902 ($65); dark brown lustre, coralene decoration, marked "Gibsons & Sons," crown and ribbon, England, no number, early-1900s ($45).

Black and brown lustre, three coralene teapots, "For England and Democracy," World War II fund-raising, marked on all three the same with Staffordshire knot, lion and Union Jack, escorted to U.S by Royal Navy or Allied Fleets ($45-$55).

From left: Two dripless spout teapots, mottled glaze, marks for "ALB," Alcock, Lindley & Bloore, England, brown teapot c1920 ($50); yellow and green c1940 ($40).

Two brown pottery teapots, same mold used, one slightly larger, smaller pot has added flowers and gold, English Rockingham style, no mark, c1920, footed bottom unusual ($38 each).

From left: Mottled brown and yellow, marked "Tundra, Canada," c1960s ($35); brown glaze, painted over glaze and wearing off, dripless spout, impressed mark "Royal Canadian Art Pottery, Hamilton, Canada, Royal Dripless," 1950s-1960s ($48).

Brown lustre coralene teapots, from left: Taller pot, marked "Made in Japan," c1955 ($18); low, squatty shape unusual, paper label on bottom "Del Coronado, Nasco Product, Japan," c1950 ($25).

Brown lustre coralene teapots, both late-1950s, from left: Ribbed pumpkin-shape marked "Japan" ($20); round shape, has unusual coralene along top edge, marked "Japan" ($20).

Three McCoy pottery teapots in the same shape, marked McCoy, U.S.A., c1957 (small are $28 and large are $35).

Rebekah at the Well teapots, from left: Brown pottery, no mark, by Morton's Pottery, c1911, Morton's made seven different Rebekah teapots ($95); lustre Rebekah, hand-painted design, no mark, possibly made in Japan, c1930 ($55).

From left: Tea seldom spoils ... Mottoware, predominantly made in Torquay, England, mark also includes the name "Watocombe," made from late-1800s to 1960s, this pot possibly 1930s ($95); two-tone, marked "Sadler, Made in Staffordshire, England," many styles and colors made with half the pot decorated, c1940s ($75).

From left: Teal green glaze on medium-sized teapot, marked "USA," c1950s ($30); dark teal, 2-cup teapot, marked "USA," c1950s ($30).

From left: Yellow glaze, 8-cup size, marked "U.S.A.," heavy pottery ($30); yellow speckled, tall shape, marked "Bauer, Made in U.S.A." ($55).

From left: McCoy, pastel Daisy pattern, 1942, crack in handle ($65); McCoy, two-tone green pattern, 1954, minor wear ($75).

Two McCoy teapots, from left: 4-cup, 1943, marked large "McCoy" ($50); vegetable motif with matte white finish, marked "McCoy & LCC" (Lancaster Colony Company), c1974 ($28).

Front, from left: Floral blue and green, marked "Made In Portugal," handpainted, c1960 ($30); back: pumpkin-shape, no mark, possibly U.S., c1940s ($28); right: crude pottery, glossy glaze, no mark, possibly individual creation, U.S. ($25).

From left: Buff sharkskin, pieces of set, made in Japan from 1929-1940s, no mark on any pieces (tea caddy $45, teapot $40, creamer $22).

From left: Pear shape with rattan handle, rim and spout glazed white, inside is brown glaze, marked "Denmark" ($85); large 8-cup, square coralene-decorated, unusual cobalt color, called Colonial shape, crudely made with pocks in the glaze, marked "Made in Japan," 1932 ($48).

Jug Town ware, buff glaze pottery, U.S., late-1920s to 1930s ($125).

Colorful bird and flowers adorn this pottery teapot, made in France, has strainer that fits inside lid, by Mousteer, c1970s ($65). (photo courtesy of Gary Stotsky, Pennsylvania)

Individual-size coralene decorated brown pottery, body is terra cotta or brown clay, marked "Japan" or "Made in Japan," 1950s ($18-$22).

From left: Yixing teapots: from left: gourd with vines and peanuts, mouse finial, smooth finish, marked in Chinese symbols on bottom, lid perfect tight fit ($55); hexagon shape with Chinese symbol, chop marks on bottom and under lid, modern ($35).

From left: Large Brown Betty, marked "Made in England," maker unknown, possibly Sadler or Gibson's ($45); Brown Betty, paper label "Genuine Old English Redware Teapot, Ridgeway" ($35).

MAJOLICA POTTERY

Majolica is a general term given today for pottery that has an overall design in relief and transparent glazes revealing the pottery texture. Predominant colors are shades of green, blue and brown with details In red, yellow or orange. Majolica styles usually include natural forms like leaves, flowers, and animals with backgrounds of geometric, basketweave or pebbly textures.

Thought to have been first produced in Italy, the name majolica (or maiolica) is taken from the island of Majorca, possibly because early pieces were produced there or it may have been shipped through this port. Majolica was first produced in the 1700s with a tin-enamel glaze to strengthen the softer porcelain of that period. Delftware produced in Holland also used tin-enamel glazing as did the Italian ware known as "Faience." As pottery and porcelain methods developed a stronger body, glazes did not need the hardening agent of tin oxide, but this style has been produced by potteries in England, Europe, Japan and the United States.

Majolica teapots made in the late-1700s and during the 1800s depicted fruit forms such as a cauliflower, pineapple, pear, lettuce, apple and even a large corn on the cob. Other teapot shapes include a bundle of bamboo, a basket of flowers and a seashell encrusted with other shells. Interestingly, English majolica was produced in the form of various types of fish. Dedicated majolica collectors watch for any of the several styles of fish pitchers and a fish eating another fish teapots produced by many companies including the well-know Minton of England. In May 1998 at the Skinner auction in Boston, one of these fish teapots sold for $32,200 (although the low estimate at the time was $1,000). The buyer is a renowned majolica collector and his overbidding represents the growing attention this pottery, which was once ignored by collectors, has been receiving.

Minton produced quite an array of majolica teapots from about 1880-1920, and the fortunate collector can find an example, especially if he or she makes a trip to England. Fine specimens are now in museums and private collections, but the style has never truly been discontinued. Majolica became especially popular during the Victorian period and pouring tea through a teapot such as a monkey holding a peach, provided not only a novelty but delightful tea time conversation.

During the late-1800s, the Griffen, Smith & Hill Pottery Company of Pennsylvania produced majolica pottery, including a tea set in the cauliflower pattern. Marked pieces of its pottery are identifiable by a circle mark bearing the company initials and the words "Etruscan Majolica."

By the 1930s, Japan potters imitated majolica teapots, and one example is an individual-sized conch shell with a rattan wrapped handle. Lovely hand-decorated and high-gloss glazed teapots were made by Maruhan in Japan. Majolica teapots were often fashioned with a flower or other interesting lid finial, continuing the design elsewhere on the pot.

Modern majolica style teapots have been produced in the last 20 years especially by Fitz & Floyd, Otagiri, Wade and other firms. During the mid-1990s, green majolica-styled kitchenware, including a teapot with a basketweave and leaf design, was marketed through well-known department stores. Collectors need to be aware of modern pieces that, while quite collectible, aren't as high in value as vintage majolica.

Many pottery and porcelain references have a section on majolica but specialists will want The Collector's Encyclopedia of Majolica by Mariann Katz-Marks.

From left: Individual size, square, crazing, glazed bisque, marked impressed made in Japan ($22); peacock, rattan handle, peacock finial, c1960, marked "Japan" impressed on bottom $25).

From left: Weller, wooded scene, Glendale or Selma, crazing, marked "Weller U.S.A." ($75); basket motif, pear says "Tea," glazed bisque, no mark, possibly Japanese ($30).

Honeycomb and bees are the motif for this pot, matching salt & pepper, other matching pieces were also made, c1950s, marked "Made in Japan" ($50 for set).

From left: Twin tea on tray, basket or weave design, flower finials, pieces marked "Made in Japan" ($45); cozy stacking set, bisque pottery, checkered basket design, flower finial, marked "Made in Japan" ($65).

Pottery Teapots

ITEM	VALUE
Blue Willow, round, squat shape, no mark, Buffalo Pottery Co.	$125.00
Brown glaze, hand-painted, rooster, metal bail handle, marked "Japan," c1960	$28.00
Cameoware by Harker, USA, solid color with white flowers, esp. blue, c1940	$75.00
Canadian, dark brown/white mottling, marked "Royal Canadian Art Pottery, Hamilton, Can."	$35.00
Chinese clay, set of 10 different colors, marked in Chinese writing, modern, each	$20.00
Citrus reamer, majolica style yellow basket weave, lid is reamer, no mark, from Japan	$45.00
Country flowers, similar to Italian pottery, hand-painted, Southern Potteries, USA	$75.00-$95.00
Crown Ducal, Colonial Times, historical views, made in 1932, marked "Crown Ducal"	$150.00
Hull, Magnolia pattern, matte glaze of pastel colors, marked "Hull Pottery," c1940s	$210.00
Individual size, kelly green, leaf finial, marked "Stangl"	$45.00
Lustre, black/gray, aladdin shape, no mark, made in Japan, c1950s-1960s	$28.00
Majolica-style, scene of travelers, bisque pottery, bail handle, marked "Hand-Painted, Japan"	$65.00
McCoy, Ivy or English Ivy pattern, large branch handle, marked "McCoy, USA," c1950	$95.00-$110.00
Medium green glaze, bud finial, Petal pattern by Mt. Clemens Pottery, USA, 1950s	$75.00
Pebble texture, bail handle of rattan/reed, no mark, made in Japan, c1930s-1940s	$45.00-$75.00
Ribbed bottom half in blue, upper white, Upico pattern, marked "Universal Pottery, USA"	$65.00
Roseville, Zephyr Lily pattern, set with sugar & creamer, marked "Roseville Pottery," c1940s	$325.00
Round shape, concentric ring decor, Fiesta by Homer Laughlin, c1940s-1960s	$150.00-$200.00
Swirl design, oblong shape, marked "Royal China" with crown, "Sebring, Ohio, USA," c1940	$65.00-$85.00
Tapered shape, triangle handle and finial, Harlequin, by Homer Laughlin, c1940s-1950s	$85.00-$145.00
Terra cotta clay, clear glaze, individual size, marked "Guernsey Cooking Ware," c1910	$75.00
White glaze with blooming clover, metal bail handle, marked "Embassy Quality Products," Japan	$28.00

From left: Boat shape, impressed "Japan" mark, modern ($25); boat shape, Bauer Pottery Co., called Aladdin, marked "U.S.A.," larger size also made, c1940s ($95).

Silver & Other Metal Teapots

Pewter, tall shape with much detail, glass panels depict Chinese tea ceremony, Chinese marking on bottom, piece connecting the long spout is a dragon ($75).

Teapots have been made of various metals for ages with the most common being silver, silverplate, pewter, brass and copper. Other types of metal teapots produced with less popularity are cast iron, chrome-plated and aluminum. While metal teapots have been produced in large numbers, they are not the best choice for steeping a pot of tea. Silver or silverplated pots are the least intrusive when it comes to metal imparting a certain flavor into the tea. Metal teapots used frequently will build up a layer inside the pot, alleviating this problem to a certain degree.

Silver and Silverplated Teapots

The term "sterling" is often used to denote silver, and it's uncertain if this term originated from German silversmiths brought to England and dubbed "Easterlings," referring to the fact that they were from the East with a gradual change to use the latter half of the word. Or if this term was derived from the term "steorra" which is old English for star and referring to the star marked on some coins.

Sterling silver has a content of 925 parts silver and 75 parts containing other metals such as nickel. The content of silver varies depending upon the country in which it was produced. Considered a precious metal, teapots fashioned in this medium are highly desired, very expensive and becoming increasingly hard to find.

The soft composition of silver teapots makes them prone to dents, scratches or damage to parts such as hinged lids. When the tarnish is shined, they are an alluring tea time vessel. The earliest known silver teapots were actually made in Holland before 1765 and imitated Chinese ceramic pots.

At about this same period, a silversmithing worker named Thomas Boulsover in Sheffield, England, accidentally found that silver could be fused to other metals like copper and brass. After 10 years of perfecting the silver plating process, teapots and other items were marketable. The town of Sheffield has been associated with silverplating ever since.

Silver teapots made in England and soon after in the New World, often had fruitwood handles or with some sort of spacers in the handle to prevent the heat transfer which makes handles become too hot. Tea sets were commissioned to be made one piece at a time, except for the very wealthy who could afford the whole set served on a matching tray. During the late-1700s and 1800s, teapots were commonly monogrammed with either the family name or letter of last name. Sometimes dates were included for special events such as a wedding or anniversary. In modern wealthy circles this practice is still followed, especially for a wedding gift with the family monogram inscribed on a silver tea set.

Today, collectors aren't as enthusiastic about

From left: Silverplate, footed, hinged lid, Arabic marking "Theieres Koutbla, Fabrique Salam," modern ($35); silverplate, footed, hinged lid, plastic finial and spacers, Arabic marking "Theiere Moulay Hassan, Fabrication Darel Berrad," modern ($45).

Silverplate, hinged lid, Bakelite handle and finial, paneled sides, marked Made in Sheffield, England, EPNS "(electro-plated nickel silver), c1930, some wear in plating ($55); silverplate, flowers on spout and handle, hinged lid, marked "By Fina," ($50).

teapots or sets with monogrammed names or letters unless they have some history that has been passed down with them. When the date is included, this enhances the value because age of the teapot is clearly defined.

Collectors specializing in silver and silverplate will find marks can be quite complicated, but there are good references for English and American silver. The New England states of Connecticut, Massachusetts, Maryland and New York founded some of the most prominent silver and silverplating companies, many of which are still in business or have merged with other organizations. Quality silver, silverplate and teapots in various metals have come out of the Meriden, CT, area. Companies such as the Meriden Britannia Company, the Manning, Bowman Co., and the International Silver Co. are a few names to be found. Unfortunately, some silver or pewter is only marked Meriden and it's hard to determine a specific company, although it designates an origin from this city in Connecticut.

Silver teapots range from $200 to $2,000, depending upon the style, decoration and any identification marks. In a mail order catalog of 1992, antique "tipping kettles" were offered, having been purchased in Sheffield, England. These are teapots on warming stands, used to serve hot water or tea. The advertised price was $1,999.95 for these silverplated, beautifully chased and engraved teapots.

Silverplated teapots are still within the financial reach of many collectors but determining if the pot is silver or silver plate can be a challenge. If the item is marked "925," it designates silver. Look inside the pot and if you find a copper or brass color, you know it's plated. Should you need professional assistance in determining whether your teapot is silver, silverplated or some other alloy, check in your local yellow pages under "silversmiths."

Pewter or Britannia

Pewter is an alloy of tin, and many combinations have been used in the last three centuries to produce varying types of this gray metal. The addition of one or more of the following may have been used in pewter: copper, antimony, brass, lead or bismuth. Pewter is generally a soft alloy but the combination of tin and antimony results in the hardest product. Bismuth might be added to this formula to add even more hardness, especially for daily-use items such as plates, bowls and teapots.

Once dubbed the poor man's silver, most pewter teapots were inspired by designs in silver. Pewter teapots were made in the American Colonies as early as the mid-1600s, flourishing into the 1800s. Unfortunately for collectors, a large amount of pewter was melted down during the American Revolution to be used for bullets, making examples

Silverplate tea set, wood handles and finials, marked "PM Italy" with horse, c1950s-1960s ($65).

Aluminum Turkish teapot has two sections, modern ($45). (photo courtesy of Gary Stotsky, Pennsylvania)

before 1775 hard to find. By the mid- to late-1800s, pottery, porcelain and china were becoming increasingly popular and teapots made of pewter declined in desirability.

Britannia is one of many formulas of better quality pewter and contains no lead. Primarily, it was tin, antimony and copper with perhaps zinc. Britannia was used following the Revolutionary War to regain the popularity of pewter. Because of this formula, Britannia could be fashioned on a lathe in a process called "spinning." Many years later, it was discovered that Britannia lent itself well to the silver-electroplating process, adding yet another dimension to this popular product for housewares (such as teapots). All of these aspects helped make Britannia fashionable in the 19th century. Identifying the marks on pewter, sometimes called "touchmarks," can be a challenge with limited sources available. Many fine pewter teapots made in England and the United States were not marked and the closest identification may be from photos in a book; even then, an absolute match may be difficult. Pewter touchmarks may only bear the name of where they were made, such as Meriden, Hartford or Baltimore, giving only a partial clue to their origin.

Collectors can find help in books on silver or silverplated items because metalsmiths often worked in more than one medium. An example of two companies that produced pewter at some point in their histories are the International Silver Company (many Britannia factories joined together in 1898 to form this company) and the Reed and Barton Company.

Pewter teapots made after 1900 were often silverplated. Although examples can be found into the 1930s, by that time, the popularity of pewter had greatly diminished. Pewter was produced in China around the turn of the 20th century although it was used more as a material for tea caddies than teapots.

Today, pewter teapots range in price from $75 to hundreds of dollars, depending on the styling, touchmark and condition. Because pewter is prone to dents and cracking, teapots in excellent condition are difficult to find. Values should reflect any imperfections. (See "Reference Section" for information on the Pewter Collectors Club).

Brass and Copper Teapots

Brass and copper teapots have been produced since the late-18th century but have never been the best choice for steeping a flavorful pot of tea. Brass is a durable metal consisting of copper and zinc and possibly small amounts of other alloys. Copper is mined from a natural ore and is one of the best conductors of heat, one of the reasons many tea kettles and tipping kettles were fashioned from this reddish colored metal.

Teapots have been made from either of these related compositions predominantly in China, India, England and the United States and to a lesser extent in other countries. Utilitarian copper was often lined with tin for durability and, if for constant use, to prevent poisoning. One of the ways to identify examples from the 18th century is the dovetailed seam where it was joined. By the

Pewter, copper wrapped handle, brass finial, marked impressed "M.H." in diamond ($35); light metal, possibly polished aluminum, handle plastic coated, unusual mark on outer rim and lid rim "RWP U.S.A." and symbol, c1940s ($45).

From left: Pewter, wood handle, hinged lid, mark is numbers, early 1900s ($65); pewter, hinged lid, hollow handle, marked "New Amsterdam Silver Co.," pewter and Nos., c1930 ($75).

19th century, joints were seamed. This determination applies to those brass and copper items made in the United States while variations existed for teapots made in other countries and even from one metalsmith to another.

In the first three decades of the 20th century, the Chinese produced brass teapots with designs in relief where colorful stones were inset or enamel coloring was applied. Marking on these pots is simply China stamped into the bottom. Tipping pots, or teapots on a stand allowing for easy tipping, were made of copper and brass. Stands were sometimes made of wrought iron where they could be placed close to a fire for warming.

Bronze is a related medium from which teapots have been formed, mainly in the Orient. Bronze is an alloy of copper and tin with traces of other metals. In modern times, a white metal is coated with bronze and this is referred to as "bronzed."

India has exported many brass teapots and the majority found on the secondary market today have been made in the last 30 years. Fashioned in the recognizable

Indian style with a tall neck and tiny spout, the question is whether tea could actually be brewed in such a pot. The hand-engraved designs on teapots from India make them alluring to collectors, but most are priced low. Modern teapots and sets imitate vintage silver styling and some even have a stay-cool handle of another material. India has produced brass items for centuries and truly antique brass will be recognizable by the exact attention to detail and a higher quality of brass, taking longer to tarnish.

In Russia, the well-known samovar was made of brass in many styles and with wood or Bakelite handles. Reproductions similar to antique versions will be distinguishable by markings. To find a samovar which includes the original small teapot atop the hot water pot is a prize for any collector.

Brass and copper teapots have been reproduced in shapes and sizes similar to antique pots and collectors must study the makers, characteristics and styles of these pots. Copper tea kettles have been made in the last 40 years which resemble earlier versions, especially those with a ceramic piece

Copper and brass, chain connects lid, fish shaped spout, snake styled handle, no mark ($45).

Small brass pot with stand, marked "R India" and paper pamphlet says "Made by Craftsmen, art handed down through the generations, India Brassware, nickel plated, hand-engraved," black iron, warming stand, coated inside, removable strainer, marked in Japanese writing under spout ($75).

From left: Copper stacking set, wood side handle, brass spout and finial, lid is a dinner bell, marked "Orfemex, Mexico, Aztec Chief" ($75); copper, globe shape with ball feet, Art Deco design, enameled finial and handle, brass accents, marked China, c1940s, some wear ($50).

in the bail handle and lid finial. In the mid-1980s, a copper-plated teapot with a gooseneck spout and wooden bail handle was filled with a floral arrangement and marketed by F.T.D. Marked with a paper label, once this identification is removed, collectors may mistake this kettle for an older version. Collectors should also be aware of copper-plated teapots. Informative references are available on antique copper and brass.

Other Metal Teapots

Teapots have been fashioned out of several other metals especially during the late-1800s and all during the 20th century. Smelting aluminum from the compound element bauxite was devised in the early-1900s, and, while some teapots were made in the 1930s, the majority were made after 1950. Aluminum teapots are usually marked and easy to identify. Quality examples have a reed-covered bail handle or bakelite handle.

Chromium (chrome) plated teapots were made by the Chase Brass & Copper Company in the 1940s. A globe-shaped teapot was available either with or without an electrical heating element and featured a plastic handle and finial. To appeal to tastes and styles of the era, chrome plating was used by other companies from 1910-1950s.

Cast iron tea kettles and some teapots are drawing the attention of collectors today with prices making a gradual increase. Because cast iron kettles tend to be large and heavy, enthusiasts desire only a representative few. Many were made to fit wood-burning stoves and stove owners search out the right fit for a burner or a match the name of stove and kettle. Kettles were used to heat water while teapots were made for the steeping of tea, so teapots of iron may have an enamel lined body. Iron teapots have been made in China and Japan and modern pots fashioned after vintage styles are still available currently.

Any of the many types of metal teapots will enhance your collection and collectors need to study older specimens and modern versions to determine authenticity.

From left: Miniature copper and brass teapot does not have removable lid, finial of glass bead, stamped simply China on bottom ($45); brass teapot with polished stone insets and applied leaves and vines design, handle is stationary, bead finial, stamped China on bottom ($55).

Top: brass, inscribed flowers and leaves, marked India incised on bottom, c1970 ($30); right: brass, bail handle, cross-hatched design, no mark ($40); left: brass, formed from ammunition shells, impressed marked on bottom with eagle, around lid, marked "Bryant" ($55).

Kettle on warming stand, small, stamped "China" on bottom, allover hand-worked design, brass, not polished, late-1800s ($175).

Spigot teapot, electrical, tea ball inside lid can be pulled out of tea to stop brewing by a chain and ball, patent numbers on base date from 1903 to 1910, marked "General Electric Company," feet, handles and finial are wood ($250).

All aluminum, all marked "Swan Brand," front, from left: 2 cups, modern handle, England ($18); made for Coronation Queen Elizabeth II, 1953, England ($35); back: 2 cups, rounded handle, England ($22).

From left: Round as a Brown Betty, this aluminum pot has riveted handle, marked "Aluminio, Fantuzzi, Fab. Chilena" (made in Chile), modern ($30); quaint pot has paneled sides, wicker on bail handle, marked "Japan" on piece holding handle, Bakelite finial has origami bird, 1950s ($30).

Golden brass tea set, pot has Bakelite handle, paper label "India," c1960s-1970s ($75 for set).

Silver & Other Metal Teapots

ITEM	VALUE
Brass, Russian samovar, privately done reproduction made in Turkey, 1980	$200.00
Brass, silver lined, kettle style on warming stand, marked "Palmer Mfg. Co.," c1889, U.S.	$250.00
Chrome-plated, dome-shape pot on a pedestal, no mark, possible Japan, c1960	$55.00
Pewter, hammered overall, wood handle and finial, marked "Sheffield, England," late-1800s	$95.00
Pewter, London shape with wooden handle and finial, marked "I. Trask," late-1700s to 1800s	$650.00
Silver, apple shape, heavy chasing, monogram, by C.T. Fox & Geo. Fox, England, 1840s	$1,500.00
Silver, bullet-style, wooden handle & finial, by Edward Pocock, London, early-1700s	$800.00
Silver, lacquered, vermeil and turquoise insets, marked "Lucien Gaillard," c1904	$2,500.00
Silver, pear shape, hinged lid, wood handle, marked "John Brevoort, U.S.A.," c1740	$750.00
Silverplated, engraved, kettle-style, on warming stand, English silver marks, c1870	$2,000.00
Silverplated, molded leaves and berries, wooden handle, on stand, England, c1890	$1,500.00
Silverplated, monogram design, marked "Meriden Britannia Co.," mid-1800s	$85.00
Silverplated, stacking set, 2-cup pot, sugar & creamer, England, modern	$65.00
Silverplated, with sugar & creamer, hammered design, marked Meriden, dated 1934	$650.00
Teaball, Art Deco style stainless steel, marked Bodum, from Denmark, modern	$175.00

Hammered aluminum (see marks in "Introduction" section for mark etched on the bottom) by Sona Ware, made in England ($45).

Untraditional Teapots

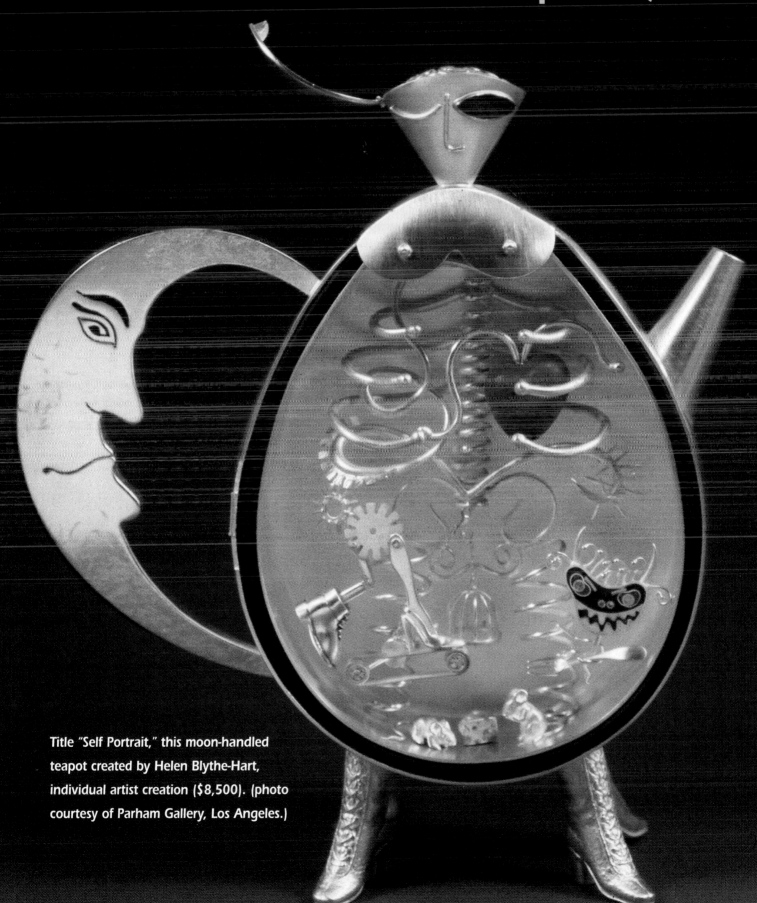

Title "Self Portrait," this moon-handled teapot created by Helen Blythe-Hart, individual artist creation ($8,500). (photo courtesy of Parham Gallery, Los Angeles.)

The term "untraditional" may conjure the idea of enchanting figural teapots but in this chapter you will discover those out-of-the-ordinary inventions, sometimes in an effort to make tea time easier, other times purely from the depths of imagination. These teapots are not as common as English floral or American pottery, but collectors may happen upon an example in their continued search of tea time vessels.

One of the earliest deviations from a traditional teapot is the S.Y.P. (Simple Yet Perfect), invented by the Earl of Dundonald in 1901. In this pot, tea leaves are held in a chamber where a lid would normally fit. After hot water is added, the pot is tipped back on little feet and its handle. The water reaches the tea leaves and steeps. When three to five minutes have passed, the pot is turned upright, the leaves stay in the upper chamber and tea can be poured. Several companies produced this teapot and the majority were done by Wedgwood in porcelain with a blue floral decoration. A Sheffield silversmith, James Dixon & Sons, fashioned a beautiful silver S.Y.P. with an ebony handle.

Why not pour two or three cups at the same time if possible? That was the idea behind double- and triple-spouted teapots. An early example is a black-glazed earthenware double-spout teapot made around 1900. In 1968, artist David Seeger took the convenience one step further to make a triple-spouted teapot. The trick is placing the cups and saucers in the strategic place for pouring from more than one spout.

A double-spouted teapot was made by the Hall China Company in the 1940s, and this version has spouts opposite of one another with one large handle going across the top. Called the Tea Master, it was made by Hall but marketed by the Twin-spout Pottery Company in two different models, both having separate chambers—one for tea, the other for hot water. With each Tea Master came an illustrated pamphlet explaining how to use this teapot which was available in 10 different shades although collectors highly desire the cobalt and Chinese red colors.

While dripping spouts and lids that fall off have long been a frustration when pouring tea from a teapot, Pountney and Co. Ltd. of Bristol, England, invented the Cosy Pot to alleviate these two problems. The Cosy pot featured a recessed lid with a straining lip which would not fall off when pouring. This pot did away with the spout which normally comes off the body of a teapot and instead placed an opening at the top of the pot. While this pot doesn't drip and the lid stays on, it was never a big enough hit to replace the traditional style teapot. This teapot was used on railroads where both of its main features were appreciated and examples can be found with the name of a rail line and scenery. Today collectors enjoy the markings on this pot and under the lid which help make it easy to identify. The majority were patented by Abram Allware Ltd. and later manufactured by Wood & Sons, Ltd.

Copper tea cozy has brass ball feet, opens from center, openings for spout and handle ($45 for cozy only). (photo courtesy of Joan Oates, Michigan)

Hammered-silver cosy is lined inside, knob and base in plastic, marked "Thermisol," cloverleaf with "SUS" in each leaf, Bauscher-Lizenz, made to fit various teapots with openings for spout and handle ($55). (photo courtesy of Joan Oates, Michigan)

The self-pouring teapot sought to make pouring easier and maybe prevent drips. This teapot's lid is pushed up and down with a vacuum-type action that causes the tea to automatically come out of a down-turned (referred to as dripless) spout. It was manufactured in varying designs by several companies with a well-known model by Royal Doulton around the turn of the 20th century.

Other innovative teapots are not quite as unique in their approach to tea time convenience. Teapots with their own cozy—a cover to keep the tea hot for a longer period—were made by Tony Wood in England, Hall China in the United States and even in Japan. The majority have an aluminum cover that is felt-lined. This cover fits over the teapot with slots to allow for the handle and spout. A modern version is available from a French company and the cozy is felt-lined stainless steel boasting that tea can be kept hot for up to one hour. Along with keeping the pot warm, cozies also keep the lid on the teapot.

The Cadogan teapot supposedly imitated Chinese wine pots and the story goes that a Mrs. Cadogan brought one to England after a visit. The Rockingham factory was requested to manufacture a similar pot. Made in several styles, the most common is a brown glazed pottery. This pot has no lid and is filled from the bottom where it enters a chamber to brew and then tea pours out the spout. While they are a novelty to look at, they are impractical for tea because the opening is so small

only loose tea leaves could be pushed into this pot and an infuser couldn't be used. This makes the teapot hard to clean—in fact one is never sure if the pot is clean.

The attempt to boil the water, or at least make it hot enough to steep tea, and brew tea in one pot has been devised by many inventors. Most of these have an electric element which is inserted into the pot and were made from the 1930s into the 1950s. One version is glass with its own infuser and others are ceramic, made in England and Japan. The notion of mixing electricity and water never went over well with tea drinkers and the pots are more a novel idea than anything else.

Teapots that travel with you on a train or to the park were devised by the Chinese in the early part of the 1900s. A padded basket with sections to store the teapot, filled with tea, and another compartment for cups, allows taking tea to be a portable affair. A wicker hinged lid has a metal closure and handle for toting. The teapot and cups are marked "China" and have Chinese writing.

An English "en route" tea basket was devised and could be attached to a railway carriage window. This basket held a metal teapot and burner, drinking glass, glass bottle shaped like a tea caddy and stacking brass containers. Not only could you have your tea en route, but obviously you could bring a lunch, the cream and maybe even some water. Drew & Sons, on London's Picadilly Circus, patented and marketed this "en route"

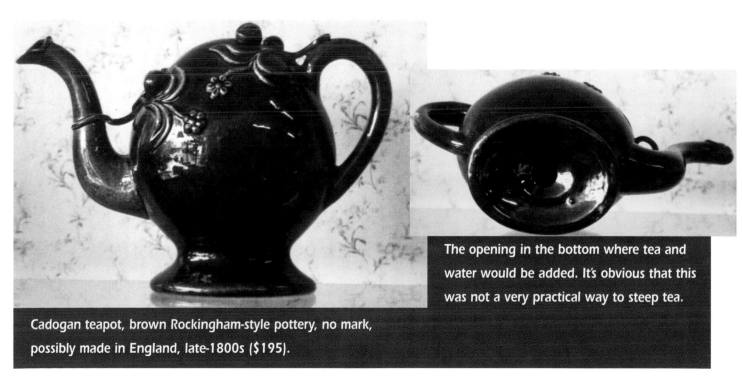

The opening in the bottom where tea and water would be added. It's obvious that this was not a very practical way to steep tea.

Cadogan teapot, brown Rockingham-style pottery, no mark, possibly made in England, late-1800s ($195).

basket that was probably also made to encourage taking the train into London for shopping.

Many attempts have been made to produce an automatic tea machine and they've either been too tedious to use or too expensive to manufacture. In 1995, the Mr. Coffee Company marketed its better half: Mrs. Tea. This tea maker heats water and then pumps it into the chamber where loose tea or tea bags are placed. The steeped tea drips into a porcelain teapot which sits on a burner plate. Mrs. Tea is quite efficient and capable of making a pot of your favorite tea, but some aficionados follow the thought that water must come to a boiling temperature of 212 degrees to steep tea properly. Mrs. Tea should not be disregarded on this account because I've shared many pots of tea from my automatic tea maker. The latest versions have timers and a new shape to the porcelain teapot.

The TeaMate by The Chef's Choice is a similar machine which makes a tea concentrate and then diffuses the infusion before pouring into the glass carafe. This product has been tested with Lipton, the Republic of Tea, Harney & Sons and other tea companies in the United States with a consensus that it's ideal for brewing black teas. This tea maker heats water to steep tea between 204 and 208 degrees and has a variable steeping time from 2 to 25 minutes.

Other companies are marketing quick tea makers that feature water raised to boiling temperatures, cordless electric teakettles (the kettle lifts off a heating element that automatically shuts off) and teapots with plunger infusers.

There's something missing on most modern tea makers—the charming characteristics of a teapot: A curving spout, sure handle and decorated body. Boiling water in a kettle and steeping tea in a nice round-bodied teapot will be the method of choice even into the 21st century, but designers may continue to try their inventive tea brewing ideas.

From left: Cosy set, rose finial, marked "Royal Winton, Grimwades, Made in England," some crazing, ($95); cosy set can either be for hot water and tea or two for two, marked "Heatmaster, Dub-L-Dekr," patent Nos., "Made in England" raised in porcelain, some crazing, ($75).

From left: Cozy covered, made by the Hall China Co., marked name and "Made in U.S.A.," cover made elsewhere, 1940s-1950s ($75); Tiffin Tea Liqueur, an unusual way to have your tea, large paper label on back of pot explains the special recipe includes the finest Darjeeling leaves, a favorite for after dinner sipping, imported by Shaw Ross Importers, Inc., Miami, Florida, U.S.A., made in Munich-Germany, cork and liqueur still in place ($150).

Traveling tea set in wicker basket, hand-sewn padding to protect pot and two cups, dragon design with gold, marked in red, China, early-1990s ($120).

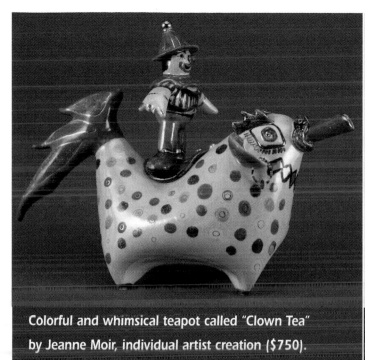

Colorful and whimsical teapot called "Clown Tea" by Jeanne Moir, individual artist creation ($750). (photo courtesy of Parham Gallery, Los Angeles)

Teapot titled "Tea Bag Nag" by Carol T. Owen, individual artist creation ($2,500). (photo courtesy of Parham Gallery, Los Angeles)

Three spouted teapot is a novelty that never became popular, Rockingham-style pottery with design in relief, was on display at Cooper Hewitt Museum 20 years ago, late-1800s, early 1900s ($2,000). (Photo courtesy of Gerald Schultz, The Antique Gallery, Philadelphia)

Spigot tea dispenser, black glaze, marked "U.S.A.," manufacturer uncertain, many potteries produced such items for soda fountains or restaurants, great iced tea dispenser ($125).

Hall China Twin Tea, soft robin-egg blue, set rests on fitted tray, marked "Hall China," set used at Rumplemyers, in one pot hot water could be served, in the other tea ($75). (photo courtesy of Gary Stotsky, Pennsylvania)

"Chili & Es ~ Tea" is a glazed ceramic teapot created by Jilda Schwartz, individual artist creation ($3,000). (photo courtesy of Parham Gallery, Los Angeles)

Set of teapots called "Whirling Dervish II" by Elizabeth Wamsley, individual artist creation ($1,000 each). (photo courtesy of Parham Gallery, Los Angeles)

Stacking cozy teapot, made in Russia, especially large size, a strong tea would be made in the upper pot, hot water kept in the bottom pot, Russian tradition is to make a strong tea and then dilute as desired ($350). (From private collection of Sylvester and Janet Carter, San Diego)

Tea dispenser, large-sized teapot with spigot made and marked "Hall China, U.S.A.," pot separate from base, c1940s ($350). (courtesy of J. Camp, LaMesa, California)

Untraditional Teapots

ITEM	VALUE
Barge, large size, teapot finial, various greetings, Staffordshire, England, c1800s-1900s	$500.00-$1,000.00
Cadogan, filled upside down, brown glazed pottery, Rockingham style, c1850	$350.00
Cozy, copper, with latch, ball feet and top knob are brass, padded, to fit any pot	$65.00
Cozy, latches closed, hammered silver-color metal, marked "Thermisol, Bausher" (German)	$110.00
Cozy, set, panels on metal covers, with sugar & creamer, marked "Sadler, England," c1940s-1950s	$75.00
Cozy, slips over pot, copper-color metal, individual size, marked "Japan," c1950	$45.00
Cozy, slips over top of pot, padded metal, earthenware pot, made in England, c1940	$55.00
Puzzle pot, not practical for tea, puzzle is how tea travels in pot, made in Japan	$150.00
S.Y.P., Simple Yet Perfect, pot lays back to brew, marked "S.Y.P., Wedgwood," c1900s	$500.00
S.Y.P., white porcelain, blue decor, marked "Oaklands, Cheswick, London, Wedgwood"	$450.00
Self-pouring, lid is pushed down, tea comes out, Royle's, by Royal Doulton, c1900	$500.00
Triple spout, white glaze with blue decor, by David Seeger, c1968	$85.00
Twin spout, spouts next to each other, brown/black glaze, made in England, c1900	$200.00

Wood tea set not functional but interesting carved detail, from Puerto Rico, no mark, 1988 ($45).

Cosy pot has ingenious lid that locks in place and has a strainer lip, marked "Manufactured by Wood & Sons, Ltd., Patented Throughout the World," includes pat. Nos., "Proprietors Abram Allware, Ltd.," late-1800s to early-1900s ($125).

Glossary

Accouterments: Equipment, trappings. Tea time equipage: creamer, sugar bowl, sugar tongs, lemon squeezer, tea strainer, tea infuser, mote spoon, teapot trivet or tile, etc.

Art Deco: A pervasive decorative style of streamlined shapes and curves, sometimes simplistic, popular during the 1920s and 1930s.

Arts & Crafts Movement: Considered to be from 1895 to 1920, a move towards hand-craftsmanship and away from mass producing, especially furniture, but this idea carried over into other areas, even teapots.

Backstamp: A printed mark, usually on the bottom of a teapot, which identifies either the country and/or company of manufacture. Commonly black, red or gold.

Basalt: A dry-bodied lightweight earthenware. Most were not glazed, although examples exist. Also referred to as redware, caneware and stoneware. Similar to Oriental unglazed stoneware.

Bisque: From biscuit, an unglazed, but fired clay. Chalky-type body.

Blue Willow: The blue version of willow ware (see Willow ware). First produced in England in 1780, later by U.S. and Japanese potteries. Transfer design, many variations exist.

Body: Referring to the color and composition of the clay.

Ceramics: The art of making an object out of clay. This term is used generally in America to refer to pottery, porcelain, china and individually formed clay items.

China: A thin, transparent or translucent material, not glazed. Painted or transferred decoration often applied.

Chocolate pot: Similar to a teapot but has a tall shape and the spout is usually more of a pouring lip with no strainer.

Circa: Approximate dating. May include 10 years either before or after the date. In this book, closer dating of 5 years either before or after is implied.

Coralene: Raised enamel dots or applied decoration over brown or black glaze. Easily chipped off during normal use. Used extensively by English and Japanese potteries from 1930s to 1950s.

Decal: A transfer type of decoration which was printed on a special paper and adhered to the glaze. When firing, the printed decoration "melts" into the glaze.

Dragonware: Japanese porcelain with air-brush style decoration and dragons either in relief or applied slip. Cups to some sets have lithophanes: when held to light can see figure. 1930s to present.

Earthenware: A heavy pottery made predominantly from earthen clay.

Enamelware: See also graniteware. Enamel coating over various types of metal on all or sections of a teapot. Easily chipped during use.

Finial: The top knob of a teapot lid. Often molded into some shape such as a flower, animal or other interesting design.

Flow blue: A blue decoration on white pottery or ironstone where the design flows or bleeds, rather than distinct definition. Watch for modern reproductions; study this category to know antique from modern.

Georgian Era: The period before the reign of Queen Victoria.

George III—1760-1820, George IV—1820-1830. Affluence was important and tea time was evidence of such.

Glaze: A transparent or opaque substance applied to pottery and porcelain, usually of mineral content and a tint. When fired, a glass-like product is formed.

Graniteware: Enamel coating over various types of metal to look like the swirls in granite. Produced in United States, England, Germany, Czechoslovakia, Poland and Japan as early as 1876.

Hand-painted: Decoration or painted design done by hand either in factory production or by china painters on blanks. Transfer printed scenes often hand-painted with various colors. Brush strokes apparent.

Hard-paste porcelain: True porcelain which is made from china clay or kaolin. Kaolin is a white clay formed from decomposed feldspar (aluminum silicate). When fired above 1350 degrees, it forms a hard body.

Jasperware: An unglazed, light stoneware made popular by Wedgwood, but produced by others, including Japan. Grecian style figures and trees applied in white relief. Body made in many colors, esp. blue.

Lustre: Shiny glaze, various colors, opalescent in appearance. Some lustres done in gold, silver or bronze by adding these metals to the glaze.

Mark or marking: The mark, usually on the bottom, of a teapot. Can be printed, incised, raised or a paper sticker.

Mochaware: Pottery made in England from 1780 to 1840 with marblized glaze. Study this category to understand antique from new mochaware which is pottery decorated on a lathe for a flowing effect.

Pottery: The place pottery, porcelain or china is produced. Also a heavy clay material, formed and fired one or more times. Often brown or off-white.

Rococo: An 18th century style which includes fanciful curves and is excessively ornate.

Salt-glaze: Originally adding salt to the firing process made a harder porcelain. Also produced a slightly pitted surface. Antique salt-glazed teapots are museum examples.

Soft-paste porcelain: Predominantly made in England's Staffordshire District from about 1820 to 1860. Also called creamware. Easily cracked or chipped.

Terra Cotta: A clay usually reddish brown in color similar to common flower pots. From the Italian meaning "cooked earth."

Transfer printed: The process of transferring a design onto the porcelain or pottery. This was done before firing so that it became part of the glazed finish or afterwards and then colors painted into the scene.

Victorian Era: Queen Victoria reigned from 1837 to 1901. The Victorian Era is considered to be from about 1850 to 1920 where fancy, frivolous and fluff were the order of the day. Victoria helped make tea time an involved ritual with all sorts of paraphernalia and beautiful pots.

Vitrified or vitreous: Meaning glass-like. A porcelain, usually containing silica, fired at high temperatures.

Ware: Reference to the composition or type of teapot, e.g. porcelain, bisque, transfer design.

Willow ware: The most popular being Blue Willow, also produced in cranberry, brown and multi-colored patterns and variations on this scene including willow trees, lovers crossing a bridge and two doves.

Yellow ware: A heavy pottery, color ranging from orangish to tan with much of it yellow in color. Made both in England and United States, mainly kitchenware and teapots are not prevalent.

Books About Teapots

An Anthology of British Teapots, Philip Miller and Michael Berthoud (Micawber Publications: 1985)

British Teapots & Tea Drinking, Robin Emmerson (HMSO, London, Crown copyright: 1992)

The British Teapot, Janet and Tim Street-Porter (Angus & Robertson Publishers, London: 1981)

China Teapots, Pauline Agius (Lutterworth Press, Great Britain: 1989)

The Eccentric Teapot, Garth Clark (Abbeville Press, New York: 1989)

Japanese Teapots, Noritake Kanzaki (Kodansha International, Tokyo, New York: 1981)

Novelty Teapots, Edward Brahmah (Quiller Press, London: 1992)

Talking About Teapots John Bedford (Max Parrish & Co, London: 1964)

Teapot Treasury and Related Items, Richard Luckin (RK Publishing, Colorado: 1987)

Teapots, Tina M. Carter (Chartwell Books, New Jersey: 1998)

Books About Tea and Tea Time

The Afternoon Tea Book, Michael Smith (MacMillan, New York: 1986)

Book of Tea, The Kakuzo, Charles E. Okakura (Tuttle Co., Vermont: 1956)

A Cup of Christmas Tea, Tom Hegg (Waldman House Press: 1982)

The East India Company Book of Tea, Antony Wild (Harper Collins Publishers, London: 1994)

If Teacups Could Talk, Emilie Barnes (Harvest House Publishers, Oregon: 1994)

The Pleasures of Tea, editors of Victoria Magazine (Hearst Books, New York: 1999)

A Spot of Tea, Linda R. Wexler (Chelsea Street Productions, California: 1997)

The Tea Lover's Treasury, James Norwood Pratt (101 Productions, California: 1982)

Books on Pottery & Porcelain

Children's Dishes, Margaret and Kenn Whitmyer (Collector Books, Paducah, KY: 1984)

Collector's Encyclopedia of California Pottery, Jack Chipman (Collector Books, Paducah, KY: 1992)

Collector's Encyclopedia of Geisha Girl Porcelain, Elyce Litts (Collector Books, Paducah, KY: 1988)

The Collector's Encyclopedia of Hall China, Margaret & Kenn Whitmyer (Collector Books, Paducah, KY: 1989)

DeBolt's Dictionary of American Pottery Marks, Gerald DeBolt (Collector Books, Paducah, KY: 1994)

English Toy China, Doris Anderson Lechler (Antique Publications, Marietta, OH: 1989)

The Fine Art of European Porcelain, Donatella Viggiani (Scott Publications, Michigan: 1990)

Korea's Pottery Heritage, Vol. II, Edward B. Adams (Seoul International Publishing House, Seoul, Korea: 1989)

Larkin China, Walter Ayars (Echo Publishing, Pennsylvania: 1990)

Lefton China, Loretta DeLozier (Collector Books, Paducah, KY: 1995)

Lefton China Book II, Loretta DeLozier (Collector Books, Paducah, KY: 1997)

Miller's Pottery & Porcelain Marks, Gordon Lang (London: 1995)

Porcelain, Cooper-Hewitt Museum (The Smithsonian Institution's National Museum of Design: 1979)

Porcelain Through the Ages, George Savage (Cassell & Company, Ltd., London: 1954)

Potter, Cooper-Hewitt Museum (The Smithsonian Institution's National Museum of Design: 1981)

Pottery and Porcelain, Harvey Duke (House of Collectibles, New York: 1989)

Pottery and Porcelain Ceramics, Kyle Husfloen and Susan N. Cox (Antique Trader Books, Dubuque, IA: 1997)

Royal Winton Porcelain, Eileen Rose Busby (Antique Publications, Marietta, OH: 1998)

Price Guides

Flea Market Trader, 12th ed., Sharon and Bob Huxford (Collector Books, Paducah, KY: 1999)

Schroeder's Antiques Price Guide, Sharon and Bob Huxford (Collector Books, Paducah, KY: 1999)

Warman's Americana & Collectibles Price Guide, 9th ed., Ellen T. Schroy, editor (Krause Publications, Iola, WI: 1999)

Warman's Antiques and Collectibles Price Guide, 34th ed., Ellen T. Schroy, editor (Krause Publications, Iola, WI: 2000)

Books on Other Subjects with Teapots

Chats on Old Pewter, H.J.L.J. Masse (Dover Publications, New York: 1971)

The Collector's Encyclopedia of Graniteware, Helen Greguire (Collector Books, Paducah, KY: 1990)

The Collector's Encyclopedia of Graniteware, Book 2, Helen Greguire (Collector Books, Paducah, KY: 1993)

Kovel's Know Your Antiques, Ralph and Terry Kovel (Crown Publishers, New York: 1981)

Kovel's New Dictionary of Marks Pottery & Porcelain, Ralph and Terry Kovel (Crown Publishers, New York: 1986)

Oriental Antiques & Art, Sandra Andacht (Wallace-Homestead Book Co., Radnor, PA: 1987)

Resources for Books, Teapots, Tea & Accessories

Antique Publications (catalog of publications): P.O. Box 553, Marietta, OH 45750, 800-533-3433, www.antiquepublications.com

British Royal Commemoratives (listing of commemoratives for sale): 6755 Coralite Long Beach, CA 90808, (562) 421-0881

Cobble Stone Cottage (tea parties, teapots, tea): 1945 Alpine Blvd., Alpine, CA 91901, (619) 445-6064

Collector Books Request Catalog (antique books): P.O. Box 3009, Paducah, KY 420021, 800-626-5420

Collector's Teapot ($2 for catalog, teapots, tea, accessories): P.O. Box 1193, Kingston, NY 12402, 800-724-3306

Emily's Gifts Teapots (specialized, private blend tea): 25414 Harper Ave., St. Clair Shores, MI 48081, (810) 777-5250, teabags@emilysgifts.com

Fleur-de-tea (mail order tea, teapots, tea accessories): 729 W. Washington St., San Diego, CA 92103, (619) 291-4TEA, www.fleurdetea.com

Irresistible Cookie Jar (catalog, teapot cookie cutters): P.O. Box 3230, Hayden Lake, ID 83835, (208) 667-1347

James Sadler & Sons, Ltd. (wholesale catalog, inquire about retail): Market Place, Stoke-on-Trent, Staffordshire, ST6 4AZ England, www.james-sadler.co.uk

John Ives Bookseller (antiques and collectibles books in England): 5 Normanhurst Dr., Twickenham, Middlesex TW1 1NA England, phone—011 441 0181 892 6265

Kitchen, Etc. (catalog of dinnerware lines with teapots): 32 Industrial Dr., Exeter, NH 038331, 800-232-4070, www.kitchenetc.com

Magnolia Antique Mall (chinz china limited edition): Joyce-Lynn, 456 N. Magnolia Ave., El Cajon, CA 92020, (619) 444-0628

Portal Market (Yixing-style teapots): 2267 Sacramento St. #2, San Francisco, CA 94115, (415) 567-9143, earthportals.com/Portal_market/tea

Replacements, Ltd. (china search service, outlet, museum): P.O. Box 26029, Greensboro, NC 27420, 800-737-5223, www.replacements.com

Sally's Place (info on tea, teapot, books): sallys-place.com

Sur La Table (catalog, kitchen items, teapots, tea): 1765 6th Ave. SouthSeattle, WA 98134, 800-243-0852

Tea Talk (quarterly, on the pleasures of tea and related): P.O. Box 860, Sausalito, CA 94966, (415) 331-1557, teatalk@aol.com

Tea, A Magazine (bi-monthly articles, tea and related): P.O. Box 348, Scotland, CT 06264, 888-456-8651

TeaTime Gazette (three issues a year on tea and related info): P.O. Box 40276, St. Paul, MN 55104, (651) 227-7415, lleamer@aol.com

Trader Joe's (tea catalog): P.O. Box 3270, South Pasadena, CA 92031, 800-SHOPTJS

UK Stuff (teapots, china, tableware): 888-857-8833, www.ukstuff.com

Victoria Fair (chintzware, tea books, Victorian items): P.O. Box 7765, Red Oak, IA 51591, 800-223-3089

Victorian Trading Company (catalog teapots, tea sets, Victorian items): P.O. Box 411342, Kansas City, MO 64141, 800-800-6647

Places to View Teapots

A. Houberbocken, Inc. (annual teapot exhibit): 230 Wells, Ste. 202, Milwaukee, WI 53203, (414) 276-6002

Bramah Tea & Coffee Museum (large collection): The Clove Building, Maguire Street, London, SE1 2NQ England, phone— 011 44 171-378 0222

Charleston Tea Plantation (tea plantation, retail shop, tours): 6617 May Bank Hwy., Wadmalay Island, SC 29487, 800-443-5987

Cooper-Hewitt Museum of Design (some teapots, inquire about special exhibits): 2 East 91st St., New York, NY 10028, (212) 860-6868

Gallery Alexander (annual teapot exhibit): 7850 Girard Ave., LaJolla, CA 92037, (619) 458-9433

George R. Gardiner Museum of Ceramic Art (two stories of porcelain and pottery, teapots): 111 Queen's Park, Toronto, M5S 2C7, Canada, (416) 593-9300

Mills College Collection (several hundred teapots): Alumni Association, 500 MacArthur Blvd., Oakland, CA 94602, (510) 430-2164

Parham Gallery (fine and exotic teapots, Saturday and by appointment): 2847 Armacost Ave., Los Angeles, CA 90064, (310) 473-5603

Trenton Teapot Festival/Veilleuses Collection (collection open all year, festival in May): 309 College St., Trenton, TN 38382, (901) 855-0973

Twining Teapot Gallery (2,600 teapots, 18th and 19th century): Norwich Castle, Stamford, England

Victoria and Albert Museum (ceramics gallery, large collection teapots): Cromwell Road London SW7 2RL 0171 938-8500, vam.ac.uk/about/history.html

Wadsworth Atheneum (177 Veilleuse-theieres, Newman Collection): 600 Main St., Hartford, CT 06101, (860) 278-2670

Information Resources

Cardew Collectors Club (collector's organization for Cardew teapots): 91 Great Hill Rd., Naugatuck, CT 06770

Holy Mountain Trading Company (articles on teapots and tea, retail source): www.Holymtn.com/home.htm